PHILOSOPHY

AN ILLUSTRATED HISTORY OF THOUGHT

PONDERABLES™
100
IDEAS THAT
CHANGED THE WORLD
WHO DID WHAT WHEN

PHILOSOPHY

AN ILLUSTRATED HISTORY OF THOUGHT

Tom Jackson

SHELTER HARBOR PRESS

NEW YORK

Contents

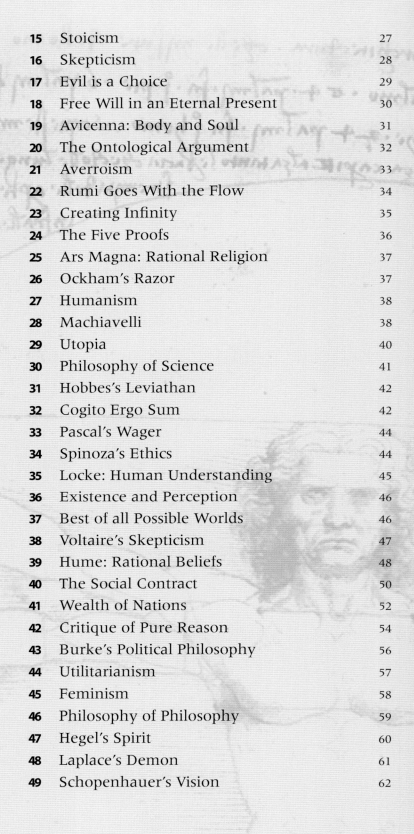

Jean-Paul Sartre's philosophy was a major influence on the protest movements of the 1960s.

Introduction

ANYONE CAN BE A PHILOSOPHER. YOU WON'T NEED SPECIAL EQUIPMENT: THE TOOLS OF PHILOSOPHY ARE IDEAS. WHERE DO THEY COME FROM? WELL, THAT IS ONE OF THE FIRST QUESTIONS A PHILOSOPHER MIGHT ASK. YOU'RE READY TO START.

The thoughts and deeds of great thinkers always make great stories, and here we have one hundred all together. Each story relates a ponderable, a weighty problem that became a discovery and changed the way we understand the world and our place in it.

Philosophy is at once the most fundamental field of enquiry and the most esoteric. Without it we would literally not "know" anything, yet it is steadfast in its focus on subjects that are beyond conclusion and asks questions that can never really be answered. To many that might make philosophy seem like a dead-end waste of time, but just a short journey through the history of philosophy can open you to new ways of thinking, give you many different ways of understanding your

own existence, and perhaps make you question how you choose to live. Without doubt philosophizing is a personal affair, although most would also argue it is impossible to do alone. It needs to be debated and communicated if only so we can see reflections of ourselves in the words and deeds of others. That is how the story of philosophy plays out in this book's pages and how it continues to this day. On reflection, you may decide that you are all alone—but, remember, that is something you share with everyone else!

Left: Diogenes the Cynic, a philosopher from the Classical Era, advocated being free from the trappings of civilization.

Left: In 1651, Thomas Hobbes pictured society as a monster, the Leviathan, that was made up of individuals but also ruled over them.

Below: In the 1920s Ludwig Wittgenstein wanted to know how it was that once you call this a duck, it can also be a rabbit.

century changed all that, as European thinkers began to revisit long-held ideas, and through the Reformation and Enlightenment, the philosophy rule book was rewritten by the likes of John Locke, David Hume, and Immanuel Kant. By the 19th century, philosophy was becoming a practical subject, with the work of Adam Smith, Karl Marx, and John Stuart Mill put to the test during tumultuous revolutions and unprecedented social upheavals. By the 20th century, philosophers reined in the more romantic notions of their forebears, applying a strict logic that threw out a lot of what had come before. Instead they now drove to reduce every word, every emotion, and every action to their most basic principles. And where will that leave philosophy in the future? Still the same questions need an answer. Let's take a look at them on the next page.

Below: If a computer could be made to think in the same way we do—it might be easier to do than we think—would that make the computer a human?

STARTING BIG
The history of philosophy did not begin by looking inward. The word *philosopher* means "a lover of wisdom," and the early practitioners, from ancient Greece to imperial China, were interested in everything. They set out to understand the Universe in the round, creating "big picture" theories that were meant to inform every facet of human life. In some respects Eastern philosophy, as espoused by Siddhartha Gautama (the Buddha) or Laozi, has continued down this path, focusing on an intuitive interconnectedness with nature. However, the Western tradition took a decisive turn with Socrates in the 5th century BCE: Socrates put aside enquiries into the nature of things. Instead he wanted to know how it is we can know something and tell right from wrong or truth from falsehood. Within a couple of generations, Plato and then Aristotle had set the scene for Western philosophy for the next 1,000 years if not more, and it is from their work that what we talk about as "philosophy" has grown.

QUESTIONING EVERYTHING
Through the European Dark Ages—so called because its history is obscure—and the bountiful Islamic Golden Age—which ran more or less concurrently and was anything but dark and obscure—philosophy was largely an arm of religion, attempting to demystify God's mysterious moves. The Renaissance of the 14th

Aims of Philosophy

Philosophy starts with asking questions, but not just any questions. There are little questions about everyday experiences, such as: What can I eat? When can I sleep? These queries take "common sense" to answer, and we've been asking them through the whole of history, from the moment we can speak. However, the common sense we use to figure them out is always changing, not only as we mature as individuals, but also as our societies have changed over the course of history.

Then there are big questions, about the natural phenomena we see around us and significant problems that we need to solve: When will the winter come? Can we cure this disease? Is it possible to improve on this tool? These questions are asked by scientists and other experts, and they are answered through making observations, collecting data, suggesting explanations, and then testing them to see if they are true.

And then there are fundamental questions, which are asked by philosophers. Some might argue that philosophy begins with just one question: What is the meaning of life? However, here we've suggested five fundamental questions to start us off. These are a good starting place for understanding the different topics philosophers ponder. The aim of philosophy is to provide an answer to questions like these. They seem simple, but people have been coming up with complicated answers for them for centuries. What are your answers?

The fundamental questions are the starting points for five major branches of philosophy.

FUNDAMENTAL QUESTIONS

What is real? ..

What can be known? ..

What should I do? ..

What is allowed and disallowed? ..

What can life be like? ..

METAPHYSICS

THE STUDY OF EXISTENCE

Many would argue that metaphysics is the foundation of philosophy. It provides interpretations of everything that is part of reality—and even questions if all of it is real. Metaphysics encompasses ideas such as cause and effect, existence, and identity and attempts to draw a line between the physical and imaginary worlds.

EPISTEMOLOGY

THE STUDY OF KNOWLEDGE

Everything a philosopher does is based on ideas, and epistemology is the study of ideas in themselves. It tackles how we obtain knowledge of the world and how we might validate it as true. To do this we must understand what role our minds have in shaping how we perceive the things beyond the body.

ETHICS

THE STUDY OF ACTION

The nature of good and bad is at the heart of ethics. An ethical philosopher attempts to find a system of ethics that can be applied consistently to any situation. Such systems consider the purpose of the "right" action and whether right and wrong are natural and fixed or synthetic and changing.

POLITICS

THE STUDY OF SOCIETY

They may not appear to do so but politicians are using philosophy all the time. Politics is the study of how ethics can be applied in a society, or group of people. This generally involves some form of social contract, where people agree to give up some of their freedoms to ensure they receive protection from the unethical behaviors of others.

AESTHETICS

THE STUDY OF ART

Finally, philosophers wonder why we prefer some things over others. Aesthetics attempts to reveal what underlies our concept of beauty, especially how it relates to art. Art is apparently unique to humans, and is our way of presenting novelties, appealing new ideas that might change our world view—and make us think again about the limits of our existence.

1 Monism: One Substance

PHILOSOPHY BEGAN WITH A SIMPLE QUESTION: WHAT IS EVERYTHING MADE OF? THE MAN WHO ASKED IT WANTED AN ANSWER THAT DID not rely on magic and myth. He was Thales, who lived in the 6th century BCE in what is now Turkey. This one man is credited with triggering Western thought as we know it.

So what is his answer? What is the principal material of the Universe, from which all other things are formed? Thales got his inspiration from the farms around his home of Miletus, a prosperous Greek port. Rain was essential for a good harvest; in fact, water was essential for all forms of life. However, water was not just one thing, it could change into ice and steam, and it was also able to flow, occupying empty spaces. These three facets—change, motion, and vitality—were the proof that Thales needed to confirm everything was made from water.

The changing seasons and changeable weather brings vital rain to the fields: A crucial signal to Thales that water was the source of life, the Universe, and everything.

One is enough

The idea that the Universe springs from a single source is called monism, of which Thales is the founding figure. Monism would be the overriding school of thought in ancient Greece and elsewhere for the next three centuries, and it would also be revisited later in more sophisticated times.

2 The Way to the Tao

THE TRADITIONAL FOCUS OF PHILOSOPHY IS ON THE PONDERINGS OF WESTERN THINKERS, BUT EASTERN THOUGHT took a different route when it came to answering the fundamental questions.

In the 6th century BCE, China was in disarray as the great empire was descending into what became the Warring States period, which as the name suggests was 250 years of conflict. The Iron-Age empire was run by a network of administrators, and as the system began to collapse, these intellectuals became brains for hire, wandering from warlord to despot, advising and organizing the affairs of the highest bidder. With no central control, each scholar just ran things his own way and this led to a blossoming of intellectual creativity among all the conquests and statecraft. Chinese thinkers began to ponder the same kinds of questions as the Greeks far to the west. Like them, they were not content with using religion as a catch-all answer. However, the result was the Hundred Schools of Thought—ideas so varied and often so contradictory that no one could master them.

The yin–yang symbol depicts how opposites such as good and bad are intrinsically linked into a whole.

Finding the way
However, one set of ideas that did make itself understood in the philosophical cacophony was *Tao te ching* (meaning *The Way and its Power*), which is attributed to Laozi (often also written as Lao Tzu). This guy is oft quoted: "A journey of a thousand miles begins with a single step" is one such bon mot, but Laozi was not a real name, it just means "Old Master." Whether Laozi was a real person remains a mystery (*see* box, right). However, the associated philosophy is very real, with an estimated 400 million people saying they place it at the center of their lives.

Taoist temples are built to complement their natural settings. Taoism, or Ðaoism, is central to folk religions in China and elsewhere in the region.

In Chinese tradition, change is a constant, cyclical component of nature, in some respect mirroring the monist concept put forward by Thales. Nothing stays the same, it is always changing from one state to another. However, all these differing states are connected parts of a whole, creating a harmonious universe constantly changing but always remaining in balance. The *Tao* is a means by which humanity, so often concerned with its irrelevant self, can stay in balance with the rest of the Universe. To do this requires peace, harmony, thoughtfulness, etc, everything one might expect in a manual for living life. But it is not as simple as that. To follow the way, one must stop trying to do the right thing. One cannot easily figure out the harmony. Instead, a Taoist employs *wu wei*, meaing "non-doing." For actions to follow the Tao, they must be performed without thought, desire, or embarrassment. Give it a "non-go."

LAOZI
Did such a man exist or is he a persona created to exemplify the teachings of many? Taoists might say he is both and neither, while historians have pinpointed a man named Lao Tan who fits the description of the "Old Master."

3 Pythagoras: All is Number

HE IS PROBABLY THE MOST FAMOUS MATHEMATICIAN WHO EVER LIVED—DESPITE BEING 2,500 YEARS OLD. And when Pythagoras was at large, the differentiation between math and philosophy had yet to be made. For him, numbers were the answer to everything.

It is easy to get the impression that everything began in ancient Greece and that before around 2,500 years ago, no one discovered anything or tried to answer the big questions. Of course, this is nonsense. More ancient civilizations, such as the ones in Egypt and Mesopotamia—especially Babylon—had made advances of their own. Pythagoras is said to have left his birthplace on a Greek island and traveled to these lands, perhaps even as far afield as India, and returned with their concepts of philosophy and math, along with a few of his own. However, his most famous contribution to human understanding—the Pythagoras theorem—was actually well known long before his birth.

In a corner

As any schoolchild could tell you, the Pythagoras theorem states the relationship between the lengths of the sides of a right-angled triangle: The square of the hypotenuse (the longest side) is equal to the sum of the squares of the other two sides. The ancient Egyptians knew that a triangle with sides of length 3, 4, and 5 would obey this relationship and form a right–angled triangle. They used such a triangle to plot the

BE A PYTHAGOREAN

Members of Pythagoras's community had to follow some outlandish rules:

Abstain from beans.

Not to touch a white rooster.

Not to pick up what has fallen.

Not to break bread.

Not to step over a crossbar.

Not to stir the fire with iron.

Not to eat from whole loaf.

Not to eat the heart.

Not to walk on highways.

Do not look in a mirror beside a light.

Not to let swallows share one's roof.

Not to leave the impression of a cooking pot in ashes, instead stir them together.

When you rise from the bedclothes, roll them together and smooth out the impression of the body.

A medieval woodcut shows Pythagoras experimenting with making sounds as he sought the numerical relationships behind music.

corners of fields on the Nile floodplain every year. However, Pythagoras's ideas went further: A right-angled triangle is just two nonparallel lines that inevitably cross at some point, which are then connected by a third perpendicular line to form the triangle. While parallel lines (which never cross) are a rather special case, the Universe is actually made up of nonparallel lines, constantly criss-crossing each other. And so to a Pythagorean the geometry of triangles and the other shapes they can create is a manifestation of the underlying fabric of nature.

In harmony

In common with other cultures, the ancient Greeks had the idea that nature was a harmonious whole. Pythagoras found that numbers appeared to be the basis of music, and what could be more harmonious than that? The story goes that he stopped to listen to the sounds of hammering from a blacksmith, and discovered that a hammer weighing half as much as another produced a note an octave higher as it struck home. He went on to conduct experiments by plucking strings of different lengths and striking vessels filled with liquid to see how the notes changed. In doing so he established a relationship between object and sound. Here was more evidence that numbers were not just the foundation of the material world, but were also intrinsic to the ethereal realm of ideas.

Pythagoras was the first person we know of to find a mathematical proof for the theorem that bears his name, but there are several other ways of doing it. Here is a simple visual proof set out in a later Arabic text.

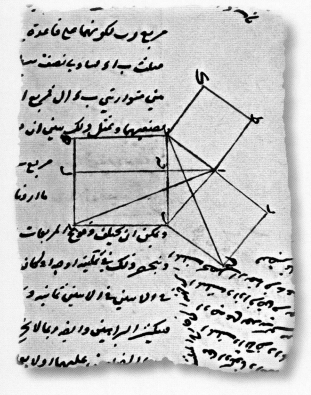

Flawed philosophy

Pythagoras set up a sect of math-minded people in Croton, Italy. They lived an ascetic lifestyle built around a reverence for whole numbers, each of which carried a certain significance: 1 symbolized reason, 2 was the undefined spirit, 3 was the sum of 1 and 2 and therefore masculine, 4 signified femininity, while 5 (2+3) was the most powerful number of all.

However, there was a flaw to Pythagorean philosophy. Dividing a square using a diagonal line makes two right-angled triangles. The length of that diagonal line (the hypotenuse of each triangle) is the square root of 2, a number that is never whole but an infinitely long decimal fraction. If something as simple, and natural, as a square did not obey the rules, why did anything else?

PYTHAGOREAN UNIVERSE

According to the Pythagoreans, the Moon, the Sun, the planets, and the stars were located in spheres that revolved around the Earth. These spheres produced musical tones as they turned. The distances between the planets had the same ratios as those that produced harmonious sounds in plucked strings. The closer spheres produced lower tones while those farther away moved faster and produced tones of a higher pitch.

A 17th-century diagram by Robert Fludd shows the hand of God, tuning up the Universe to play the "Music of the Spheres."

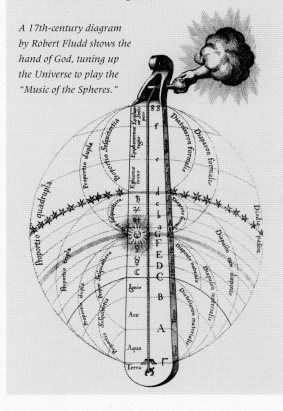

4 Buddhism

YOU MAY HAVE HEARD IT SAID THAT BUDDHISM IS "NOT A RELIGION, MORE OF A PHILOSOPHY." In fact it is something in between, where adherents follow "the Middle Way" revealed in 6th-century India.

The divergence between Eastern and Western philosophy is made apparent by Buddhism, which has its roots in India around the same time that Pythagoras and other Greek thinkers were pondering big questions around the Mediterranean. Both traditions sought to find answers that did not rely on religion. In the West religion was largely based on the poetic retelling of the Greek myths, epic stories of gods, demons, demigods, and mortal heros battling it out to establish the world order. In South Asian civilizations, the prevailing religion was Hinduism based on the epic stories of another clan of gods and monsters set out in ancient texts called the Vedas.

Greek philosophers were not content with the answers supplied by the Homeric myths. Buddhism, as founded by a 6th-century preacher called Siddhartha Gautama, was also a challenge to traditional Hindu dogma. Now comes the divergence: Western thought seeks to define the Universe and man's place within it using reason and evidence, pondering the nature of time and space, infinity, and the differences between body and soul and life and death. Siddhartha refused to be drawn on such questions, preferring to set them aside as unanswerable. He described them as a net that draws a person in and traps them in a tangle of theories and guesswork.

The Middle Way

In early life, so the story goes, Siddhartha was something of a playboy, enjoying a life of luxury and boundless pleasure. However,

FOUR NOBLE TRUTHS

Dukkha: The truth of suffering
Suffering and existence are the same thing. From the moment of birth, life is a struggle for survival, filled with pain and fear.

Samudaya: The truth of the origin of suffering
The reason why we suffer is because we have desire for pleasures of all kinds, from pleasant sensations to acquiring possessions and power over people.

Nirodha: The truth of the cessation of suffering
By giving up our cravings for pleasure, wealth, and power we will be freed from suffering.

Magga: The truth of the path to the cessation of suffering
The Eightfold Path is the way to rid yourself of suffering and dispense with selfish behaviors.

There are few if any historical figures with more statues than the Buddha. He is generally shown with big earlobes, because Siddhartha wore disks inside his ear lobes until he renounced possessions, and his pierced ears have hung low ever since.

he was unsatisfied, especially when confronted with the suffering of those around him. He chose to cast off worldly possessions and live a life of self-denial. But that was equally unsatisfying. He reasoned that the pleasure he sought in his early life served as a mere distraction from suffering. However, his second ascetic lifestyle was just suffering, because he denied himself the distraction of pleasures. He concluded suffering was the basis of existence: You suffer as you seek to quench your desires for pleasure and possessions; you suffer when you fail to do so, and even if you succeed in fulfilling a desire, the pleasure is fleeting and you suffer as it leaves you. Siddhartha, therefore, set out to navigate between suffering and pleasure to find true happiness. His teaching of this Middle Way earned him the title of the Buddha, meaning "the enlightened one," and his methods are known as Buddhism.

In life, the Buddha was a Nepalese nobleman called Siddhartha Gautama, who became an itinerant preacher.

Ending attachments

The Buddha made no claims to being a prophet or receiving guidance from some supernatural entity. His teaching has a more philosophical footing. To travel the Middle Way requires you to stop desiring things. It is desire that causes suffering. However, desire is part of human nature, so just renouncing pleasure and possessions is not enough. Instead we must detach from the self. The Buddha reasoned, in line with the Tao of Laozi, that the self was only part of a greater whole, or non-self. Any action we make (ourselves) is the effect of a previous cause from the wider non-self, and the effects of our actions are therefore a facet of the ever-changing but harmonious nature. Getting attached to the actions and effects of the self is what leads to our suffering.

On a practical level, the Buddha set out the Eightfold Path as a means of reaching enlightenment, a code for ethical living that will make us happy. The Eightfold Path leads ultimately to nirvana, sometimes seen as akin to the western idea of heaven, but better understood as transcending the self and realizing the eternal truth.

"Drop by drop is the water pot filled. Likewise, the wise man, gathering it little by little, fills himself with good."

THE BUDDHA

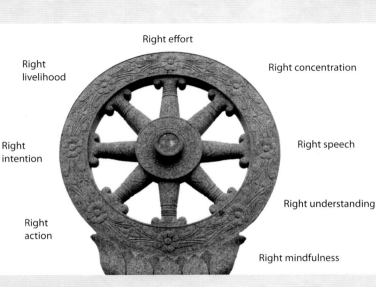

Right effort

Right livelihood

Right concentration

Right intention

Right speech

Right action

Right understanding

Right mindfulness

DHARMACAKRA

The dharma, the path to enlightenment, is often presented by a wheel, known as the *dharmacakra*. Generally a dharma wheel will have eight spokes, representing each of the principles of the Eightfold Path. The circle represents the perfect whole of the dharma, while the hub represents meditation, the core discipline in following the path. The rim represent *samadhi*, the composition of mind required by the teachings. Some wheels have more than eight spokes, often 12, 24, or 31. These numbers also have significance in more in-depth aspects of Buddhist philosophy.

5 Confucianism

BORN IN A LAND OF FREQUENT WAR AND TURMOIL, CONFUCIUS WANTED TO DEFINE MORALITY IN ITS OWN TERMS, AND THUS create a code of universal ethics that would lead to a more just and peaceful world.

Confucius's secular philosophy has meant he has remained at the center of Chinese thought, throughout the country's tumultuous history.

Born a generation after Laozi, Confucius belonged to a class of scholarly administrators and magistrates that was emerging in China at the time. These were the world's first civil servants, who sought to apply some order to the many independent and often warring states that were appearing as the early Chinese empire fragmented. The rulers of these fiefdoms believed they were mandated to lead by the gods. However, their scholarly advisors had de facto power, not through divine intervention but by the application of their wit and wisdom. It was against this background that Confucius developed his moral philosophy based on self-evident truths, rather than the entrenched traditions of monarchy and priesthood.

ANCESTOR WORSHIP

The importance Confucius placed on family loyalty has become integrated with the ancient practice of ancestor worship in China. As well as maintaining respectful relations in life, families maintain shrines in order to ensure happiness in the afterlife.

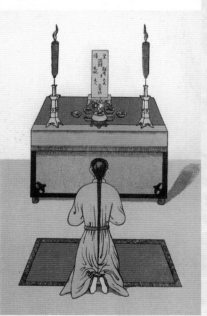

Virtue for all

Confucius's main book is his "selected sayings," or *Analects*. Much of this is expressed as aphorisms, such as,"What you know, you know; what you don't know, you don't know. This is true wisdom." However, within these pithy phrases is a system of ethics that is not beholden to class and religion. Confucius does not do away with god, or a supernatural force, altogether, but he says that we humans represent this force on Earth. Therefore, any and all people can be virtuous, irrespective of their social standing and without the say-so of gods.

Confucius was not advocating doing away with the class hierarchy, either, quite the opposite. Instead, he stressed the importance of virtuous relationships between all members of society. To do that, one

FIVE CONSTANT RELATIONSHIPS

1 Ruler and subject 2 Father and son 3 Husband and wife 4 Elder and younger 5 Friends

needed to behave in four ways: Be loyal, respect family ties, observe social rituals and good manners, and finally reciprocate good relations. These four values were applied in accordance with the social heirarchy—some relationships trumped others, as espoused in the Five Constant Relationships (above).

The most significant relationship was the political one between the ruler and the ruled. The ruler should be just and kind, in turn those who are ruled would be loyal. The same kind of reciprocal relationships were seen in order of decreasing importance between the generations, spouses, siblings, and finally between equal friends.

6 Heraclitus

WHILE HIS FOREBEARS ARE OFTEN DESCRIBED AS THE FIRST SCIENTISTS AS WELL AS THE FIRST PHILOSOPHERS, Heraclitis was very much in the second group.

"You cannot step twice into the same river." "The way up and the way down are the same." These sayings have a ring to them of the Tao and dharma of Eastern philosophies. But they were uttered by Heraclitus, a 5th-century BCE philosopher from Ephesus, a port up the coast from Miletus, the home of Western thought. While the monist traditions of Milesian philosophy were based on gathering evidence from natural phenomena, Heraclitus introduced the idea of *logos*, an over-arching idea or law that governed nature that was arrived at through the power of thought alone.

Heraclitus is sometimes dubbed the Weeping Philosopher. By all accounts he was an unhappy man, whose work was frequently interrupted by depression.

Constant flow
Much of what Heraclitis said mirrors the ideas of change and impermanence present in the Eastern philosophies being developed at the same time elsewhere in the world. He recognized that nature was a balance of opposites, and that this balance was achieved by constant changes. One transformation—the way up—was simultaneous to its opposite—the way down—resulting in what Heraclitus described as the "upward-downward path." Poetic as it was, Heraclitus's world view was soon challenged.

7 Parmenides: All is Illusion

HOT ON THE HEELS OF HERACLITIS CAME PARMENIDES, A MUCH MORE STRAIGHTFORWARD MONIST, who employed exquisite logic to reveal that the natural world is nothing but an illusion!

Parmenides relied on logic to produce a superficially illogical result.

We are on safer ground with Parmenides, who employed sensible logic to overturn the mysticism of Heraclitus—but where does it get us? Let's start at the beginning: Parmenides assumed that if something exists, it cannot not exist at the same time—logic won't stand for it. Therefore, nonexistence is impossible. Things just are, and because things cannot come from nothing, the material world has always existed, permanently. Logic then dictates that permanent things cannot change, by definition. Therefore change is impossible, and the ebb and flow of nature that we appear to experience is just an illusion under which is hidden a constant, indivisible oneness.

8 Zeno's Paradoxes

ACCORDING TO PLATO, ZENO OF ELEA WAS A YOUNG CONTEMPORARY OF PARMENIDES WHO HAD A KNACK OF SHOWING JUST HOW MISLEADING the world of our senses could be.

Plato reports thirdhand (via Aristotle) a story purportedly told to him by Socrates, when Parmenides (an old man) and Zeno (a middle-aged man) visited Socrates (a young man) in Athens. During their conversations, Zeno delighted Parmenides with ingenious paradoxes, which backed up the elder man's deduction that the changes seen in nature—especially motion—are in fact illusions hiding a motionless constancy.

Zeno is reported to have produced dozens of examples, mostly with the same theme, but only five have survived. We'll take a look at two of the most famous. The Dichotomy Paradox says that for an object to travel a given distance it must first travel half that distance, and before that a quarter, an eighth, and so on to an infinite number of divisions. The result is that this journey with an infinity of steps can never be completed. The story of Achilles and the Tortoise has a similar message. The famously athletic warrior is racing a tortoise, to which he gallantly gives a head start. Despite running

Who's going to win? If the speedy Achilles cannot beat a tortoise, shouldn't we question our understanding of motion, or whether it exists at all?

much faster than the reptile, Achilles can never win. He covers distances more quickly, sure, but when he arrives at where the tortoise was when Achilles began to run, the shelled opponent has crept on a little to a new position. And when Achilles gets there, the tortoise is further on still—he just can't catch up. He must complete an infinite series of actions in a finite amount of time: Getting halfway first requires getting half that distance but that requires first getting halfway to there... ad infinitum. When Diogenes (*see* page 25) heard these paradoxes, he just got up and walked away...

9 Atoms and Emptiness

HOW COULD A CONSTANTLY CHANGING UNIVERSE, RETAIN ITS PROPERTIES WITHOUT BEING AN ILLUSION? The answer has a rather modern ring to it: Atoms.

The chief proponent of the philosophy of atoms was a man called Democritus (but he actually got the idea from his teacher, Leucippus). He developed the idea of atoms to refute Zeno's and Parmenides's assertions that the changes witnessed in nature were illusory. For material to move, they said, it must travel into a place where there was nothing—and how could nothing change into a "thing"? And how could dividing matter result in a "nothing" occupying its place? For Democritus it was simple: Matter could not be divided indefinitely. Instead all things were constructed of tiny indivisible and eternal solids, termed *átomos*, meaning "uncuttable." Any changes in nature were merely due to atoms being rearranged. Democritus reasoned that atoms need not be identical but had characteristics that could explain the variety of substances that he observed in nature: Sticky or hooked atoms clustered into solids, while smooth ones flowed past each other in water and wind. Democritus had no evidence for his idea, he just thought it up. It was Albert Einstein in 1905 (2,300 years later) who finally provided direct evidence that atoms exist.

Democritus is styled the Laughing Philosopher (in contrast to Heraclitis).

10 Socrates: An Examined Life

SOCRATES LEFT NO WRITINGS AND OFFERED NO THEORIES TO THE WORLD. HOWEVER, HIS LIFE AND WORK MARK A CHANGE IN THE DIRECTION OF WESTERN THOUGHT: No longer were philosophers trying to explain the world at large, but they were seeking to explain how humanity should behave within it.

A conversation with Socrates would have been frustrating. The only thing he ever agreed with is his oft-quoted statement: "I know one thing: I know nothing." This skeptical approach to public life earned Socrates admirers and detractors alike. Among the admirers was Plato, from whom we get most of our information on Socrates. Among his detractors were the ruling class of Athens, who eventually were so incensed by his activities that they sentenced him to death! How could a man who just talked end up in such trouble?

These ruins in southern Greece mark one of the most sacred spots in the ancient world, the oracle at Delphi, where priestesses were said to predict the future. The Delphic oracle declared that Socrates was the wisest man in Athens— he replied that he didn't know anything at all.

Examining everything

In middle age, Socrates was wealthy enough to pursue his passion, to be a philosopher. He did not search for answers about big subjects like the nature of the Universe or the nature of material. He was interested in the virtues and vices that people use to describe themselves, such as good, bad, courage, and justice.

SOCRATIC DIALOGUE: COURAGE

Socrates wants a definition of bravery, one aspect of goodness, and approaches Laches and Nicias, two Athenian generals.

Laches: To be brave is to stand and fight.

Socrates: How can you be brave when you are not fighting?

Laches: Bravery is endurance.

Socrates: For bravery to be a form of good it cannot contradict prudence. Sometimes it is prudent— and still brave—to not endure, but withdraw.

Nicias: Bravery is knowing what is to be feared and hoped for.

Socrates: Does that mean animals have courage? Can a pig be brave?

Nicias: No, the brave require a wisdom that very few people have.

Socrates: Being fearful is to expect a future evil and being hopeful is expecting a future good. If bravery requires an understanding of future good and evil it must also involve an understanding of good in the past and present. Your definition is really a general point about knowing good and evil, and that contradicts the assertion that courage is about understanding only future events. Therefore, the definition must be false.

The discussion ends in confusion.

An 18th-century canvas by French painter Jacques-Louis David, shows Socrates still talking as he prepares to drink the hemlock—and he appears to be the person the least disturbed by the events unfolding.

He professed to knowing nothing about any subject, and his research took the form of asking questions, the so-called Socratic Dialogue. He would seek out the person seen as the most expert in a subject—for example, he would discuss bravery with soldiers—and then engage them in discussion. His technique was to use a line of questioning that exposed that what they thought they knew was based on false assumptions.

In one such exchange, Socrates talks with Phaedrus, an aristocrat with an interest in mythology. Socrates asked if the gods know everything. Phaedrus said that they must, because they are gods. Socrates then gets Phaedrus to agree that gods sometimes argue with each other about what is good or bad. That, says Socrates, means that one of the gods must be wrong on occasions and therefore cannot know everything.

Socrates came to the conclusion that the wisest men in Athens only thought they knew things—but like him, they knew nothing. The men of standing that he interrogated were invariably left confused and often offended by their encounter with Socrates. Socrates is said to have given special attention to the Sophists—tutors and rhetoricians—who charged for their services. To Socrates, they were frauds using clever words to pass on false knowledge. "There is only one good: Knowledge; and only one evil: Ignorance," he explained. Branding the most eloquent people in Athens as evil, and by association all those who used their services as well, cannot have helped Socrates's reputation among the ruling class of Athens.

SOPHISTS

Chief among Socrates's enemies were the Sophists, a group of skilled orators working in Athens. They are sometimes likened to commercial lawyers—no one really liked what they did but were unable to get things done without their help. Sophists were professional arguers. To them everything was relative—if it could be argued well enough it was true. In Socrates, this powerful bunch found an amateur arguer who time and again proved their statements to be untrue.

Condemned to death

After many years of being a philosophical thorn in the sides of Athen's elite, Socrates was put on trial. The charge was "corrupting the youth and not believing in the gods," encouraging younger people to break with tradition and question their elders and betters. Everyone on all sides assumed Socrates would agree to end his one-man philosophical crusade, and retire quietly. However, Socrates refused, declaring, "The life which is unexamined is not worth living." With that he chose a death sentence. According to Athen's laws, this was suicide by poison, and Socrates willingly drunk a fatal dose of hemlock.

11 Plato's Cave

THE STUDENT OF SOCRATES AND THE TEACHER OF ARISTOTLE, PLATO HOLDS A VERY SIGNIFICANT POSITION IN THE STORY OF PHILOSOPHY. His teachings would reappear many times over the centuries, frequently merged with religious ideals. His message was simple: We all live in the dark.

The first we hear from Plato, he is retelling the story of Socrates, his great mentor, who was put to death by the Athenians after making a career out of pricking the pomposity of members of the powerful ruling class. Plato used Socrates's own method—dialogues—to relate his master's feats of mental dexterity. In fact most of what we know about Socrates was written by Plato, so it is likely that there is more than a little bit of Plato mixed up in the persona we remember as Socrates.

PLATO'S ACADEMY

The word *academy*—and its derivation, *academic*—have their roots in a school Plato set up. Plato gathered his students in a sacred, walled olive grove outside of Athens at a place called Akademia. At first it was an informal get-together of wealthy young men, but by the year 380 BCE, it was a formal school with fee-paying pupils. One of the first alumni was Aristotle, who went on to set up his own rival college, the Lyceum.

PHILOSOPHER-KING

In Plato's book *Republic*, the philosopher set out his plans for a perfect political system. He believed the human soul was in three parts: Desire, emotion, and reason. In his city, peasants were driven by desire. The warrior class were dominated by emotion, while philosophers alone were in control of reason. The king of the city could only be a philosopher.

A scrap of manuscript from Plato's book, originally titled Politeia, *meaning "government."*

Being ideal

Plato also used dialogues to advance his own theories, and often employed a character called Socrates in these stories. However, Plato wanted to go deeper than Socrates (whoever he is). The older man was interested in how to be good, while, before he tackled moral questions, Plato wanted to understand what it was that actually existed and what were the products of the mind.

He began with physical objects. Take a cup, for example. All cups have certain agreed characteristics which make them cups, but none are the same. Some are a closer match to our ideal of a cup, others are further away—they might leak, for example. But all cups are different and none are a perfect fit with the ideal cup form, which we compare them against in our minds.

The ideal of a cup, therefore, says Plato, existed in itself in a heavenly realm and can be understood only through reason, never through the senses. We can also use reason to understand other ideals, or Forms, that don't exist in the world of the senses. For example, a circle is a shape with an outer edge that is always the same distance from the center. We know this to be true, even though we can never draw a perfect circle—it is always a bit off somewhere. Plato named the things that we could understand through reason, "Forms," and said that the world of Forms was the true reality. The world presented to us by our senses was a mere shadow of the truth. Forms were unchanging and perfect, while the senses gave the illusion of change.

In the dark and light

Plato used his Theory of Forms to describe human consciousness in the Allegory of the Cave. Humans are born with no understanding of Forms, he said. He compared this to a person being born in a cave, shackled in some way so they can only see the dark back wall of their prison. Between them and the cave entrance is a perpetual fire, and the cave dwellers grow up only ever seeing shadows on the wall, shadows of Forms cast by the fire. Plato, as a philosopher in command of reason, had been able to unshackle himself and turn to regard the Forms directly. Anyone who stayed facing the wall could only have an opinion about the world. In contrast, a philosopher, freed by his reason, knew the truth.

Forms were not just cups, circles, and other physical objects. They included the abstract virtues, such as good and bad, justice, and beauty, which again could only be truly understood using reason. But how could someone who only knew what they saw in the cave understand the truth, having never been exposed to it? Plato's answer was a bit of a fudge: Knowledge of Forms was innate; it was part of the immortal soul, which resides in the world of Forms. Philosophers have been pondering that point ever since.

A painting from 1604 CE shows Plato's Cave, with the ordinary folk destined for a life of ignorance, while the philosophers stand around knowing the truth, and offering a word of guidance to those less endowed with reason.

Plato was not an egalitarian. He advocated a political system where only philosophers (like him) could make decisions— using reason to ensure justice prevailed.

12 Aristotle's Empiricism

HAVING SPENT 20 YEARS BEING TAUGHT BY PLATO, ARISTOTLE GREW DISSATISFIED WITH THE THEORY OF FORMS. HE WAS NOT INTERESTED IN CHASING ROUND IN CIRCLES inside the heads of men. Instead, he based his philosophy on what evidence he could gather through observation.

ALEXANDER, BEFORE HE WAS GREAT

Aristotle's father was the royal physician to the king of Macedonia in northern Greece, and Aristotle was appointed tutor to a teenage heir to that throne. His name was Alexander. Aristotle taught him and his friends for about three years. Once king, his student conquered most of the known world, becoming Alexander the Great.

Aristotle described the workings of a diving bell in one of his books. As this Islamic painting shows, Alexander is said to have had a go.

Aristotle was undoubtedly a bright boy when he arrived at Plato's Academy as a teenager. Plato would have taught him his Theory of Forms, and there are hints in Plato's later writing (a dialogue called *Parmenides*; he frequently used old philosophers as characters) that something or someone was giving him doubts about the veracity of his life's work. When he died, Plato did not appoint Aristotle as his successor, and this is perhaps why: His young student did not believe in Forms, explaining his objections with the idea of the "third man." If men, in Athens and elsewhere, were representations of a Form of Man, why isn't there a Form of the Form of Man (that's the third man)? Why don't Forms have Forms themselves? And what's to stop Forms of Forms having Forms? Where does it end? To Aristotle that was enough to end his attachment to Forms.

Natural inclinations

Instead, Aristotle took his inspiration from a certain connection with nature. He was one of the first biologists, cataloging and classifying wildlife by their observable attributes. After all, it is these features that make something what it is and differentiate it from what it is not—everything else. Aristotle felt we had to rely on what we saw or sensed in other ways, and this approach, known as empiricism, was to be the basis of his theories.

However, Aristotle wanted to understand universal truths, such as what it was that kept nature together, despite its constant flux. He extrapolated his experiences of figuring out what an animal or plant was and was not to explain how we can come to understand all things.

> *"The roots of education are bitter, but the fruit is sweet."*
>
> ARISTOTLE

Experience is all

Aristotle rejected Plato's suggestion that knowledge was innate, prefigured but hidden from those who did not seek it. Instead, he argued we are born knowing nothing and learn by experiencing the world. We learn to differentiate plants from animals, fish (like dolphins) from birds (like bats)—Aristotle got a lot wrong—and man from other animals. In the same way we learn right from wrong through trial and error, and recognize justice and beauty through experience.

Aristotle formalized a system of logic, the first of its kind, to ensure that his observations were correctly classified. Known as the syllogism, it works like this: If As are Bs and C is an A then C is also a B. If fish swim and a dolphin swims, then a dolphin is a fish—so you see how it works; perfectly well unless your assumptions are incorrect.

13 Diogenes the Cynic

Aristotle believed that events had a moral aim, or final cause. This powerful idea, that nature has a purpose, still resonates today, and was an important concept in European religion as depicted in this 16th-century image, the Great Chain of Being—God is at the top.

DIOGENES LIVED WHAT HE BELIEVED, AND HE BELIEVED THE BEST LIFE HE COULD LEAD WAS TO SIT IN A BARREL. The son of a rich banker, who renounced worldy possessions, Diogenes was the first countercultural rebel.

Alexander the Great is said to have offered Diogenes charity while on a visit to Corinth. All the philosopher asked for was that the emperor move out of his sunlight!

Diogenes was the original Cynic, a word derived from the Greek for "dog." In this context the Cynics were not jaded and critical as is today's interpretation. Instead, the philosophical Cynics reject social norms so you can live in a natural state (like a dog).

Humor was very much part of Diogenes's teaching. In one story among many, he was captured by pirates and sold to a slaver. When asked his trade, Diogenes replied that it was governing men and that he should be sold to a man who needed a master.

As for his central message, Diogenes said the good life was to be free, and not to be worried about social embarrassment. And that is why he moved into a barrel, wore rags, and ate onions discarded from the market. In his words: "The happiest person has the most when they are content with the least."

14 The Original Epicurean

BEING A PHILOSOPHER AFTER THE DAYS OF PLATO AND ARISTOTLE MUST HAVE BEEN HARD. In their opposing ways, the two giants of the Classical era had pretty much sewn up the arguments. What was left to debate? Epicurus decided to just have a nice time.

Where Plato and Aristotle were concerned with the nature of existence, a field known as metaphysics, Epicurus's philosophy was more focused on ethics. He was asking how people should live. He thought that the goal of life, the moral purpose, was to be at ease, free of worry, in other words to be happy. The pursuit of happiness, in his view, was the pursuit of pleasure. In modern time, this approach has been misinterpreted as a licence to seek only sensual pleasures, chiefly in the form of fine food, intoxicating substances, and sex. However, Epicurus was no party animal. He saw the greatest pleasure in making friends and learning new things from them. He summed it up as, "It is impossible to live a pleasant life without living honorably, and it is impossible to live honorably without being pleasant."

Epicurus was no hell-raising pleasure seeker. He found happiness in living without fear.

Epicurus's work came against the backdrop of Greek mythology, in which the god Thanatos was said to torture the dying and the dead because of their sins in life.

Fearing the end

Epicurus reasoned that the biggest barrier to a pleasant life was the presence of fear. All fears stemmed from the same event—death. For people to be truly happy they had to overcome their fear of death. One reason to be unafraid of death is to think that life continues after it. However, Epicurus argued that whatever happened after death, one thing was certain: Life had ended. In death, the sensations and reason that make up life would cease. It was the end of your ability to experience or feel anything, and you have no consciousness of your condition. What is there about death to be afraid of? Epicurus lived a long life (although one plagued by ill health). Writing on his deathbed on his last day of life he described how happy he felt.

15 Stoicism

AROUND THE SAME TIME THAT EPICURUS WAS PURSUING HAPPINESS, ANOTHER ETHIC WAS BEING DEVELOPED, which took a different approach: Human beings have no influence over their lives. The best tactic is to be indifferent to it all.

This school of philosophy is called Stoicism and its founder was Zeno of Citium. Zeno had started out in his education as a Cynic, following in the footsteps of Diogenes. Zeno's philosophy had little regard for metaphysical questions. He was content to believe that nature obeyed a set of immutable laws put in train by the gods. People had no say in these laws and had no control over them whatsoever. Therefore, from the point of view of the natural order, a person enjoying pleasure and wealth should be considered in the same way as someone suffering pain and poverty.

Zeno of Citium was a chief among Stoics. He taught his philosophy under a portico of columns, known in Greek as stoa. *So he and his students became known as the Stoics.*

Rough with the smooth

To be a Stoic, Zeno taught that one should be indifferent to all experience, good or bad. In that way, a person's life would be virtuous, meaning it was in harmony with natural laws. Despite these laws being beyond the control of humanity, Zeno still believed that the course of a life was not predestined. A person could choose to be absorbed in things that they had no control over or they could choose to be Stoic. Zeno's teachings found a wide audience. Even today the word stoic is used in the same way he meant, although it generally refers to someone who endures misfortune without complaint. We seldom say that someone who is unimpressed with good fortune is being stoic—but Zeno would have.

MARCUS AURELIUS

A Roman emperor in the 3rd century CE, Marcus Aurelius is regarded as an important Stoic philosopher. As an all-powerful emperor, Marcus Aurelius wrote guidance to himself to keep him good. The work was titled *To Myself*, and renamed *Meditations* after his death. Here is one of his thoughts: A cucumber is bitter. Throw it away. There are briars in the road. Turn aside from them. This is enough. Do not add, "And why were such things made in the world?"

16 Skepticism

PHILOSOPHY'S PRIMARY PURPOSE—AT LEAST IN ANCIENT DAYS—WAS A GUIDE TO LIFE TO HELP PEOPLE ESCAPE UNNECESSARY FEAR AND WORRY. As a young man, Greek philosopher Pyrrho traveled the world, and in later years formulated his answer—nothing really mattered.

As the most powerful man in Greece, and soon the world, Alexander the Great was seldom alone. He had been educated (most famously by Aristotle) alongside his youthful friends, known as his companions. When he set out to conquer the known world, many of the companions went with him, along with other young aristocrats looking for adventure and glory. Pyrrho was one such follower, traveling with Alexander's army, absorbing all the culture and knowledge he could along the way. The empire that Alexander created reached from Greece to the Indus Valley in what is now Pakistan. It was there that Pyrrho studied under the gymnosophists, a sect of naked philosophers, who advocated the simple life.

Great doubt

After Alexander's death, some companions rose to be emperors and kings in their own right, such as Ptolemy, whose descendents ruled over Egypt for centuries. However, Pyrrho had other ideas. He returned to his home city of Elis and adopted a simple lifestyle, living out his philosophy by example rather than writing it down. (He left no books and we have few written accounts of his life.) Pyrrho was a *skeptic*, from the Greek word for "doubt." He asserted that since the senses could not be relied on (just as Plato and others had explained), we could never figure out anything about anything. Therefore, one way of life was as good as any other. The key was not to be concerned about which one. Pyrrho's travels taught him that following local custom was all that was needed—believing in a philosophy behind your actions was not required.

In this German painting from the 16th century, Pyrrho sits comfortably in a ship stricken by a storm, while all around him panic. The philosopher is tranquil because he cannot know if the ship will sink or remain afloat, so why worry?

> *"That honey is sweet I refuse to assert; that it appears sweet, I fully grant."*
>
> PYRRHO

17 Evil is a Choice

AS THE OLD POWERS OF GREECE AND ROME FADED, THE INFLUENCE OF THE CHURCH TOOK THEIR PLACE. God appeared at the center of everything, including philosophy.

Augustine's most influential work was The City of God. *This illuminated version shows the Last Judgment where God divides the sinful from the faithful.*

By the 4th century CE, the basics of Christianity as we know it today had become established. Philosophy began to explore the nature of God, and one leading figure in the early Church tackled the thorniest problem of all. Augustine of Hippo (in what is now Algeria) was curious about the nature of sin, asking how people could do evil. If God is entirely good, why did he create evil in the first place? And if he is all-powerful why doesn't he use his power to eradicate all evil for good—literally.

MANICHEANISM

Augustine ended his life as a Christian archbishop and then became a saint after death (all saints are dead), but he spent his early adulthood as a Manicheanist. Followers of this religion believed in the teachings of Mani, a Persian prophet who preached in the 3rd century CE. At the time Manicheanism rivaled Christianity, which was still a young religion, but it is now extinct. It states that God has an equal evil opposite, Satan. God controls the soul and Satan works through the body—and the world is a product of this pair's ongoing struggle for eternal dominance.

Absence of good

In his answer, Augustine made a very significant statement. He said that evil is a lack of good, not an opposite version of it. That idea has resonated through Western thought ever since. Evildoers are those who do not follow the path set out by God. Some Christians believe that the Devil exists as a supernatural being set on making people do wrong, others suggest that the Devil is a personification of humanity's ability for evil. From whichever viewpoint, God is still the most powerful entity, and evil exists because he chooses to allow it to.

Augustine reasoned that evil exists because God created humans to be rational and so by definition we are free to choose to follow God, and to be good or not. The Bible teaches that Adam himself chose to sin and thus started the whole sorry history of humanity.

18 Free Will in an Eternal Present

WHEN A ROMAN ARISTOCRAT WAS THROWN INTO JAIL BY A DISGRUNTLED GOTH CONQUEROR, he began to question what it meant to be free. Even if he were released from prison, would he really be free?

The front page of the Consolation of Philosophy, _the book in which Boëthius advocated being "philosophical" about the trials of life — such as being sentenced to death for a crime you didn't commit._

Boëthius was a Roman in the days when that no longer carried as much weight as it once did. The once great empire was crumbling, and Rome itself was overrun by the Ostrogoths. Despite an unkind view of history that these people were savage barbarians, the Goths were in many ways just as cultured as their Roman forebears, and Boëthius, a scholar and expert in classical philosophy, was appointed as advisor to the Goth king Theodoric. However, his political career ended in a death sentence for treason. While awaiting execution, he wrote the _Consolation of Philosophy_ to cheer himself up. In the book he converses with an angel-like figure, known simply as Philosophy, who consoles him for his misfortune. People have little influence over the events of their lives, she says, but what they can control is their attitude to what life throws at them.

SCHOLASTICISM

Boëthius is said to be the first Scholastic, a field of study that was centered on translating and critiquing the works of Aristotle and other classical philosophers. The work of these Greeks thinkers was regarded as more or less infallible until the 16th century.

This university lecture in the 14th century would have focused on Greek philosophy.

Free to choose

Boëthius wants to know whether he had any freedom to change the course of his life. If God is all-seeing and all-knowing, surely he knows the course of future events just as well as past events? In other words, he is timeless and eternal and knows what every person will do—good and bad—throughout their lives. If a deed is already known by God in advance, how can a person choose to do something different? Surely our freedom to choose is an illusion? Our deeds, including the sinful ones, are predestined.

God is aware of every moment in history, and the deeds contained in each one, Philosophy agrees. However, the crucial point to realize is that being a timeless entity, God does not differentiate between the deeds that have already taken place from those that have yet to be done. To him they all occur in an eternal present; he does not watch our lives develop through time. He leaves us to choose our actions for ourselves. God is interested in the choices we make—and will judge us by them—and to do that he gives us free will to make them.

19 Avicenna: Body and Soul

PLATO THOUGHT THE SOUL WAS ETERNAL, ARISTOTLE CLAIMED IT died with the body. Avicenna approached the problem by imagining what it would be like to be in a body without senses.

Avicenna thought that the soul went to paradise after death. However, that put him at odds with Islamic teaching, which states that the body ascends to heaven as well—as seen here with the prophet Isa (better known to Christians as Jesus) on the way up.

Avicenna, or Ibn Sina, was an Islamic scholar, but he was not defined by his religion. His main interest was the teachings of Aristotle, and his works on the subject were hugely influential on the Scholastic traditions of Europe, which in many ways took its lead from the academic pursuits of the Islamic world. Scholastics were not meant to disagree with Aristotle, just iron out the inconsistencies that kept cropping up as history rolled onward.

Avicenna was not just interested in the soul. He was also an expert in the body, and his books on medicine were in use for 700 years.

However, Avicenna was not happy with Aristotle's concept of soul, which he placed subordinate to the body, saying it ceased to function after death. The Persian philosopher took a position closer to that of Plato, who thought the soul (he divided it into three parts) was a separate thing to the body. To prove this Avicenna imagined himself as the Flying Man.

No sense

The Flying Man was blindfolded, ears plugged, and suspended by some force or other in midair. His arms and legs were held away so he could not touch any part of his body. He has spent his entire life like this. Despite never sensing anything, Avicenna felt sure that if he were the Flying Man, he would have had a sense of himself. That self exists separately from the body—it does not need to know it even has a body associated with it.

This thought experiment completely removes the body from the mental picture, and so Avicenna reasoned that the mind, or self, or soul, cannot be produced by the body and must be distinct. That makes Avicenna a dualist: He believed our existence arose from two parts—one that thinks and one that does.

20 The Ontological Argument

A being than which no greater can be conceived.

GOD IS ALL POWERFUL, THE MOST POWERFUL THING THAT IT IS POSSIBLE TO IMAGINE. JUST THINKING ABOUT HIM IS ENOUGH TO MAKE HIM EXIST. So says the famous argument put forward by Italian theologian St. Anselm. But if that works for God, why can't we imagine anything else into existence?

Ontology is the branch of philosophy which tackles the nature of existence. St. Anselm's Ontological Argument approaches this subject by attempting to prove the existence of God, the being that is said to have brought everything else—the whole of Creation no less—into existence. In just one step the saint's philosophy is meant to explain everything.

ANSELM AND THE FOOL

Even a fool, when he hears of a being than which nothing greater can be conceived understands what he hears, and what he understands is in his understanding… And assuredly that, than which nothing greater can be conceived, cannot exist in the understanding alone. For suppose it exists in the understanding alone: Then it can be conceived to exist in reality; which is greater…

Therefore, if that, than which nothing greater can be conceived, exists in the understanding alone, the very being, than which nothing greater can be conceived, is one, than which a greater can be conceived. But obviously this is impossible. Hence, there is no doubt that there exists a being, than which nothing greater can be conceived, and it exists both in the understanding and in reality.

Playing the Fool

St. Anselm set out his argument in *Proslogion*, a book from 1078, in which he has a conversation with the Fool, who represents a nonbeliever; in a modern context he would be an atheist. The Fool's role in the book is to be a sounding board for St. Anselm to bounce his argument off. The argument begins with a definition of God: God is the most powerful being imaginable, the greatest being that you can think of. The Fool agrees—atheists have the same definition of God as the faithful.

Existence is best

Next St. Anselm asks the Fool to agree that the idea of God—the greatest being that can be conceived—exists in his mind. The Fool agrees, the idea of God exists there, but there only. Now St. Anselm makes his big move: Is something that is only in the mind better or worse than something that exists in reality as well. As any fool would, the Fool falls into the trap. Yes, he agrees that to exist in reality is greater than to only exist in the mind. A painting that is only imagined by an artist gets better once it has actually been painted.

Ah, says St. Anselm, therefore the greatest being you can imagine cannot be limited to the mind. One can imagine a greater being that exists in the mind and in reality—and this must be the God that we are all thinking of. Just imagining God means that he exists. And everything else exists because God created it.

St. Anselm appears in many stained-glass windows in churches in England, where he served as the Archbishop of Canterbury at the end of the 11th century.

Imagine that

Not everyone was happy with St. Anselm's proof of God. Gaunilo of Marmoutiers wrote *On Behalf of the Fool* to argue the other side. He replaced the "greatest being" with a Lost Island, a perfect paradise somewhere out in the oceans. Did just imagining such a place mean it existed? Put another way why doesn't imagining the most perfect sandwich, ice cream, or bongo drum bring them into existence? St. Anselm had an answer: The Lost Island was the most perfect of a large number of islands. The argument doesn't work for things created by God—ice creams, bongos, etc.—and only works for God because he is the greatest/most perfect thing of all things.

21 Averroism

TREADING A PATH BETWEEN PHILOSOPHY AND RELIGIOUS DOGMA IS DIFFICULT. IN THE 12TH CENTURY, THE ARAB SCHOLAR AVERROES attempted to relate the truth revealed by God to the truths proposed by philosophy.

The cathedral in Córdoba, Averroes's hometown, is known as the Mezquita and was a mosque before it became a church. In a similar way, Averroism became a European philosophy despite its Islamic origins.

Ibn Rushd, Latinized into Averroes, was born in Córdoba, now in southern Spain, but at the time one of the most advanced cities on Earth and a powerful center of Islamic culture. By day Averroes was a lawyer, but by night he transformed into a radical philosopher and scientist, writing copious commentaries on the works of Aristotle. His work caught the attention of the caliph, who appointed Averroes as an official in his royal court over in Morocco.

Averroes did not find favor within his own Muslim society, but had a big impact on European philosophy. Most pictures of him appear in Catholic paintings, such as this detail from a church in Florence, Italy.

Two truths

The philosophical task Averroes set himself was to reconcile the teachings of the Koran with the teachings of Aristotle. To him, Aristotle's was the literal account of the Universe, while the Koran contained a poetic truth, which was occasionally at odds with the direct evidence of nature. However, there was no contradiction between the two schools of thought. Those who were educated enough could interpret the Koran's poetic truth so it tallied with the Aristotelian view. The untutored poor should only be presented with the Koran because it was easier for them to grasp.

The thorniest problem Averroes had to deal with was the nature of the soul: Immortal in Islam, but not according to Aristotle. Averroes opted for the Islamic position—to deny it would have invited execution. However, he linked it with Aristotle's concept of active intellect, where truths are immortal and exist outside the minds of those who think them.

22 Rumi Goes With the Flow

BEING A POET, A MYSTIC, AND A TEACHER AS WELL AS A PHILOSOPHER ENSURED THAT HISTORY REMEMBERS RUMI. Despite being a figure from the 13th century, his philosophy has a rather modern ring to it: All you need is love.

With the full name Jalal ad-din Muhammad Rumi it is little wonder that this Persian scholar is better known as simply Rumi. He was the most influential figure in Sufism, the mystical tradition of Islam. Sufism is a long tradition dating back to the start of Islam itself, but Rumi's interpretation of it, which he developed after moving to Turkey in his youth, has remained dominant to this day.

DERVISH

The Mevlevi Order of Sufism, founded by Rumi, went on to develop the Sama ceremony, better known as the Dance of the Whirling Dervishes. Dancers in traditional flowing robes and fez-like hats perform spinning dances that symbolize a Sufi adherent, or dervish, taking the spiritual journey to perfection.

One with God

Rumi's world view was based on the idea that all things are in a constant flow as they are seeking to join a universal divine oneness—in other words, to join with God. Adam's disobedience that led to the Fall of Man was the moment when the human soul became disconnected from God, and we have been trying to be reunited ever since. The force that drives the flow, Rumi characterized as love. This is not the romantic love of Hollywood movies, but an acceptance of the force of good that underlies the Universe.

A person's life was part of the divine flow. At death, their spirit was not lost but returned in another form. Rumi did not see the flow as a cycle, but an endless series of birth, death, and rebirth. There was therefore no need to fear death or loss. To understand our place in the great scheme of things, Rumi advocated deploying the emotions, not reason. This was best achieved through music, poetry, and dance. Rumi's followers carried out a series of rituals with the aim of losing themselves in love.

Contrary to mainstream Islamic practice, Sufis often build shrines and monuments to historical figures, such as this one in Shiraz, Iran, in honor of the Sufi poet Hafez.

23 Creating Infinity

IN THE 13TH CENTURY, A DEBATE RAGED ABOUT WHETHER THE UNIVERSE HAD ALWAYS EXISTED OR WHETHER IT HAD BEEN CREATED AT A CERTAIN INSTANT. That debate still goes on today, but one Italian monk thought he had the answer.

ARISTOTELIANISM

The philosophy of Aristotle influenced the work of later philosophers for many centuries. Thomas Aquinas had a simple answer for cases when Aristotle's teachings contradicted Christian dogma: God created Aristotle, so his reasonings could not be wrong. They only appeared to contradict the word of God because Aristotle had been alive before Christ, and so the truth about God had not been revealed to him.

As well as being a clergyman, Thomas Aquinas was a philosopher in the Scholastic tradition and so the two great inspirations for his work were Christian doctrine and the teachings of Aristotle. Aristotle had said that the Universe had always existed; there was no time when the Universe had not been there. However, the book of Genesis describes how the Universe is brought into existence by God. So which was it?

Scholastic philosophers had gone along with Aristotle, but that put them at odds with religious teaching—something not to be encouraged in the Middle Ages. In any case, earlier philosophers had found a flaw with Aristotle's argument. Could it be possible that the great philosopher was actually wrong?

Absolute infinity

The argument against an eternal Universe went like this: Aristotle had said that the Universe would go on for an infinite number of days, and had already existed for the same length of time. In ancient Greece, infinity was a touchy subject. Actual infinity, where an infinite number of things exist all at once, was deemed beyond the scope of man, and left in the realm of the gods, and thus Aristotle said that it was impossible. However, an infinite time was possible as a "potential infinity" because days occur one at a time. If that was the case, the detractors argued, the number of immortal human souls which had been accruing during the infinity of Earth's past would constitute an actual infinity, thus contradicting Aristotle's own argument.

Aquinas dismissed this opposition to Aristotle. God was all-powerful so it was perfectly possible for him to create an eternal Universe. He had done so at some moment in the past, as the Bible and other holy books claimed, but God created it to have an infinite past and infinite future. And so in the instant of creation, the Universe had always existed and there was no time when it did not exist as Aristotle had stated. Aquinas's mastery of logic meant that both viewpoints were completely correct!

Aristotle, being long dead before Jesus arrived on Earth, had no concept of the Holy Trinity. But Aquinas argued that was not to say Aristotle disagreed with the idea.

24 The Five Proofs

HAVING COMBINED THE WORKS OF ARISTOTLE WITH CHRISTIAN DOCTRINE, THOMAS AQUINAS WENT ON TO OFFER THE QUINQUE VIAE—THE FIVE WAYS or five proofs of God. The proofs were meant to be an empirical way of approaching religion, removing the need for spiritual revelation.

The five proofs grow out of the question: Where did the Universe come from? If you can answer that, you will have revealed the nature of God, or so Aquinas claimed. The Universe, he explained, is a sequence of constant change and motion, a string of causes and effects, and the first proof is that of the "unmoved mover." An object cannot move by itself; it requires a push from another moving object. That "mover" in turn had been set in motion by an earlier push, and this motion can be traced back through time.

1 The Proof from Motion
2 The Proof from Efficient Cause
3 The Proof from Necessary vs. Possible Being
4 The Proof from Degrees of Perfection
5 The Proof from Design

Between 1265 and 1274, Thomas Aquinas wrote his proofs of God in a book called Summa Theologica *—the Compendium of Theology.*

But motion must have started at some point. If it had no start what makes the chain of events the way it is? God, therefore, gave the first push, creating movement without the need for an earlier mover—he is the unmoved mover. Next Aquinas uses a similar argument on cause and effect: God was the "uncaused cause" that gave rise to the first effect, which went on to cause another, and so on. Proof three discusses how objects are "possible"—they may exist at some point but may not at others. The Universe cannot be entirely composed of possible objects because that opens the possibility that there may be periods when the Universe contains nothing at all. Therefore, there must be an infinite "necessary" object that is always there, and that's God. Number four says that some things are more perfect than others, but such comparison is meaningless unless there is a perfect benchmark. That's God all over. Finally, in the fifth way, Aquinas deploys Aristotelian teleology, the idea that everything in the Universe has a purpose and is heading toward a final state. Objects have no concept of their goal, and so the Universe must be guided by an intelligence that can see where it is all headed.

25 Ars Magna: Rational Religion

AFTER CENTURIES OF RELIGIOUS CONFLICT IN SPAIN, RAMON LULL DECIDED to create a philosophy that would use logic to combine all religions.

In the Middle Ages, Spain was the frontier between the Islamic and Christian worlds. Lull, a Christian monk himself, grew up surrounded by Islamic culture, and devised a complex method for comparing and contrasting the three great Western religions—Islam, Judaism, and Christianity—which were all based on the same fundamental truths. He hoped this work, contained in his 1305 book, *Ars Magna* (*The Great Art*), would convince Muslims and Jews that is was the logical thing to do to become Christian, and so end religious conflict.

Ramon Lull is shown having a religious epiphany in this 14th-century manuscript, which looks rather like a modern graphic novel.

26 Ockham's Razor

WHEN PICKING AN ANSWER TO A PROBLEM, THE SIMPLEST ONE IS PROBABLY THE RIGHT ONE. THIS IS A MODERN TAKE on Ockham's Razor, a mental blade that cuts away superfluous thinking.

Alexander the Great (right) cuts the Gordian Knot. This story is symbolic of an intractable problem which is solved by cutting away the complexity in a somewhat brutish parallel to Ockham's Razor.

The razor is named for William of Ockham, a 14th-century English philosopher, but his contribution to the idea was one among many. The Romans called the idea the canon of parsimony, while it was Thomas Aquinas who really nailed it a century before William, saying: "It is superfluous to suppose that what can be accounted for by a few principles has been produced by many." He used it when discussing the Five Proofs of God. It was not until the 1850s that the principle was named Ockham's Razor. The technique has many applications, and is a frequent tool in philosophy to this day.

27 Humanism

KNOWN AS THE "PRINCE OF THE HUMANISTS," DESIDERIUS ERASMUS WAS A LEADING VOICE AGAINST THE RESTRICTIVE traditions of Scholasticism. Instead of learning about Aristotle and a strict set of old ideas, he advocated a wider range of subjects, such as literature and history—subjects still known today as "humanities."

Erasmus, a Dutch theologian and humanist, was not content with criticizing the blinkered Scholastic movement. He turned his ire against the Catholic Church as well, poking fun at the corruption of the clergy in a famous book called *In Praise of Folly*. This book from 1509 did much to stimulate dissent against Catholicism, and is seen as one of the catalysts for the Reformation. Soon after, Martin Luther and others called for Christians to break with the Catholic Church controlled by the Pope and join "protestant" churches. The key differences were that Protestants do not believe that God's forgiveness can only be received by a confession to a priest: All that is required is a personal faith in God. (They also rejected humanity's free will and said that those with faith were predestined to reach heaven.) However, despite calling for church reforms himself, Erasmus opposed Protestantism and remained a Catholic.

Despite many schools and colleges taking his name, Erasmus said that acquiring knowledge did not lead to happiness; if anything it did the opposite.

28 Machiavelli

FEW PEOPLE MAKE SUCH AN IMPACT THAT THEIR NAME BECOMES AN ADJECTIVE, BUT AN ITALIAN POLITICAL PHILOSOPHER ACHIEVED JUST THAT. To be Machiavellian is to lie, cheat, and even kill to achieve your aims.

THE PRINCE

Machiavelli presented his famous political philosophy in a book called *Il Principe*, meaning *The Prince*. Some people think it was meant to flatter the rulers of Florence so they would give Machiavelli a job. Others suggest the book is actually a subtle satire of the cruelty of the Medici family.

Niccolò Machiavelli came from Florence, a city-state in central Italy which was ruled by the Medicis, a family of bankers. At the turn of the 16th century, Florence and the region was in upheaval, and the Medicis had lost control of their city as other powers tussled to control Italy. During this time, Machiavelli was a diplomat, shuttling between cities, brokering alliances. However, when Florence allied with the French who subsequently lost to Spanish armies fighting for the Pope, Florence came under the influence of Rome. The Medicis were reinstated as the Pope's puppet ruler of Florence, and Machiavelli was cast into the political wilderness, without a job, influence, or the hope of advancement.

Appealing to power

In an attempt to get back into government, Machiavelli wrote a political philosophy, *Il Principe*, and dedicated it to the Medici family. It told the story of a prince who used all the tricks and techniques in winning and keeping power that Machiavelli had picked up in his years observing the work of rulers. His biggest influence was Cesare Borgia, a supremely powerful and equally terrifying overlord working for the Papacy (his dad was the Pope!), who had died a few years before the book was finished.

Cesare Borgia, a truly ruthless leader, was the closest match in real life to Machiavelli's prince. Borgia is said to have ordered a general to quash a rebellious region, which he did with great violence. Once the rebellion was over, Borgia had the general publicly executed for his crimes. That one act made people both grateful to and fearful of him.

STUDENTS OF MACHIAVELLI

The fascist regimes of the 20th century learned a lot from statecraft outlined by Machiavelli. In Italy itself, Benito Mussolini ruled for 20 years by ensuring his people loved and feared him. It was often said that he made the trains run on time, so never mind that anyone opposing him was imprisoned. As he was securing power over Iraq in 1979, Saddam Hussein ordered a meeting of national officials and read out a list of names—who were led out of the meeting, one by one (most were killed). Those that remained were congratulated on their future loyalty. Soon after Saddam killed his best friend, Adnan Hamdani. If he was seen to kill those dear to him, it was clear he would have no problem doing the same to enemies.

Machiavelli explains that a good leader cannot follow the same morality as a private individual. If a ruler acted morally they would soon be usurped by a new leader who did not. Instead, the prince should have no qualms about doing whatever he can to ensure he holds on to power. In other words, the ends justifies the means. That was not as simple as just killing all his enemies; the prince should be loved and feared equally by the people. That is the achievement of a true Machiavellian, to know when it is correct to act immorally (kill, betray, lie, cheat, etc.), but also know when such an act will result in more problems than it solves. So it is normally best just to kill a few of your enemies—and frighten off the rest.

Machiavelli was not actually Machiavellian himself. His book was no doubt meant to ingratiate him to the Medici, who already practiced much of what Machiavelli preached. In a second book, *Titus Levy*, Machiavelli argued that a republic was better than a monarchy— but in times of uncertainty, a strong leader was needed.

Machiavellianism was born in Florence, a city that fostered great art, literature, and science, but was also a center of tyranny and oppression.

29 Utopia

AT THE START OF THE 16TH CENTURY, THE AMERICAS WERE A "NEW WORLD," RIPE FOR EXPLORATION AND discovery. In 1516, an English philosopher imagined finding an island there with a perfect society.

The man in question was Thomas More, a lawyer and politician during the reign of Henry VIII, England's famous king who married six wives—and beheaded two of them along with hundreds of other people who fell from his favor (including, eventually, More himself).

More called his fantastic island Utopia—a play on words which can mean both "no place" and "good place" when translated from Greek. More's book describes Utopia as a crescent-shaped island off the coast of Brazil (only recently discovered), which had been cut off from the mainland by a man-made channel. There were 54 Utopian cities, each divided into four boroughs, and home to 6,000 households— totaling around 75,000 people. Every 30 households elected a representative, called a syphograntus. Every ten syphogranti then elected from their number a traniborus who administered the 300 homes. The syphogranti also elected a prince to rule the city. A prince stayed in post for life, unless the syphogranti decided to remove him.

The population of Utopia was heavily controlled. People were sent away from overcrowded areas to set up cities on the mainland. Foreigners were allowed to join these colonies. When the population of the island fell below optimum levels, the colonies were disbanded and everyone went back to Utopia.

Utopia was inspired by the idea of a paradise on Earth. The word paradise *arises from the Persian word for "walled garden" and similarly More put his Utopia on an isolated island.*

RELIGIOUS CONFLICT

Utopia was a very liberal place, especially about religion. However, Thomas More was a devout Catholic and persecuted Protestants while Lord Chancellor of England. As the Reformation gathered pace throughout the 16th century, the religious wars and genocides made Europe anything but a utopia.

St. Bartholomew's Day Massaccre in Paris in 1575, saw Catholics kill Protestants.

Thomas More eventually got his head chopped off by Henry VIII for not approving of the king's divorce and remarriage to Anne Boleyn.

If you are thinking life in More's Utopia was a bit restrictive, you are right. Private ownership was not allowed. Food and other goods were stored in government warehouses. Households requested what they needed. There was no suggestion of shortages, although everything was rationed. Logically, this system meant that no one stole anything, and locks were not allowed on houses. Every ten years families moved to a new house. Anyone who committed a crime would become a slave for life.

It was compulsory for both men and women to work on farms for two-year stints. Everyone was also apprenticed into a trade to make the things the cities needed. Everyone wore the same clothes, houses had a standard design, tradespeople were not required to innovate, and no one had more or higher quality possessions than their neighbors. Administrators and, of course, the leaders (like More) were an elite selected from the cleverest children.

While many aspects of Utopian life were imposed by the law, citizens had the right to choose religion, which was unheard of in 16th-century Europe. The island had several religions which worshiped the Moon, Sun, planets, ancestors, and a supernatural god, and none was dominant and all were tolerated. The toleration of ideas—religious, philosophical, or political—was protected by a prayer recited by all Utopians, where they asked for the true god to let them know when they are mistaken.

30 Philosophy of Science

A LAWYER WORKING FOR HENRY VIII'S DAUGHTER, ELIZABETH, MADE ANOTHER contribution to philosophy—the scientific method.

Aristotle wrote a book of logic titled Organon (The Instrument). *Francis Bacon set out his work in* Nova Organum (The New Instrument).

SKEPTICAL SCIENCE

Within less than 50 years, Bacon's scientific method was having tangible results. Robert Boyle questioned the mystical teachings of alchemists and put chemistry on a more logical footing based on evidence. The result was the first gas law: Pressure goes up when gases are compressed. This was the first step in a long road to reveal the atom and quantum physics.

In 1620, Francis Bacon set out a system of logic which he contended was more effective than the syllogisms set out by Aristotle and other Greek philosophers. The Baconian method started with a reduction of the problem to describe it in the simplest possible terms. Next Bacon suggested doing away with syllogisms altogether. Their type of deductive logic arrives at truth by combining two premises. For example: 1) All men die; 2) Francis Bacon was a man, therefore Francis Bacon would die. Deduction works fine as long as the premises are correct, but one error leads to a cascade of further mistakes (e.g. substitute 1 for "all men fly"). Bacon suggested using inductive reasoning instead. In this case, an explanation is proposed for an observed phenomenon. Unlike deduction, the proposition is not automatically regarded as correct, but must be strengthened by seeking evidence for it, ideally through a test. Bacon's work had huge influence as the rallying call for the Scientific Revolution that was to come.

31 Hobbes's Leviathan

THOMAS HOBBES BELIEVED THAT HUMANS WERE ENTIRELY SELFISH AND COULD ONLY LIVE TOGETHER IN HARMONY thanks to the control of the state.

Despite being, by all accounts, a polite and humble man himself, Thomas Hobbes thought that given the chance, people would naturally lie, cheat, and kill to get what they wanted. This same self-interest when combined with a fear of death made people form into societies. It was only a "social contract" with a sovereign power, where individuals agreed to give up some freedoms to receive protection from each other, that prevented life being a short and violent affair. Hobbes characterized the state as the Leviathan, a powerful entity composed of individuals but wielding power over them. Hobbes believed morality stemmed from the Leviathan. People did not possess souls and were complex physical machines that behaved purely in self-interest.

The Leviathan looms over the world in Hobbes's book from 1651. The giant's body is made up of people, who support the sovereign at its head.

32 Cogito Ergo Sum

RENÉ DESCARTES WAS A TRUE GENIUS WHO LEFT MANY SIGNIFICANT LEGACIES, BUT THE PHILOSOPHY HE IS MOST remembered for is summed up by the epithet *Cogito ergo sum*—"I think, therefore I am."

René Descartes could not help but be skeptical about what he learned from his teachers as a boy at France's leading Jesuit school. As a young man he set out to find at least something that he could say was undoubtedly true—and failed. He had been a sickly child and not a strong man, and spent a lot of his time in bed. The story goes that he woke up one day only to do it again—his first awakening had been a dream. That got him thinking about how he could be sure he was awake now. Perhaps his whole life so far had been a dream from which he would awake

CARTESIAN COORDINATES

Descartes is also the inventor of graphs which represent algebraic equations as lines. It is said he got the idea of what is now called Cartesian coordinates while watching a fly buzz across a ceiling.

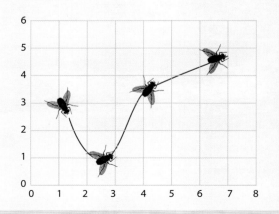

DUALISM

Descartes was interested in how the mind and its thoughts were related to the outside world of "real" things, as described and classified by science. He argued that the mind and body were made from different things, a concept now named dualism.

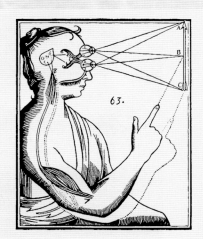

Descartes' diagram shows his theory that the senses were connected to the mind via the pineal gland.

at any moment. Unsurprisingly, he was full of doubt, and that doubt became his strongest tool.

Method of doubt

He developed a method for finding truth. If there was the slightest hint that something might be untrue, then this doubt was enough to discount it. Descartes found that he doubted his every sensory perception. Everything he saw, tasted, and touched was the product of a process that he did not understand, and so he had to doubt whether what his senses told him was real. Descartes accepted that his entire life and everything he had learned from it might be in some way a distortion of the truth, perhaps under the control of a demon, some kind of supernatural being. He did not put great store by this idea as being actually true but he nevertheless knew it was a possibility. So was there anything that he could know for sure? The fact that he was doubting every facet of his self and the world meant that at least his mind (if not his body) must exist. That was beyond doubt. While the hypothetical demon could alter reality, it could not make a nonexistent entity doubt its own thoughts (it would have no thoughts to doubt). Only something that exists can think, and only thinking things can doubt themselves. Descartes put it this way: *Cogito, ergo sum* meaning, "I think, therefore I am."

René Descartes (standing at the table right) was the tutor of Queen Christina of Sweden, a position that would kill him. The queen insisted that lessons begin before dawn and liked to keep the windows open to make it uncomfortable for her courtiers. Descartes was so exhausted by the experience that he caught pneumonia and died.

33 Pascal's Wager

IF YOU HAD TO BET ON WHETHER GOD EXISTED, WHAT WOULD YOU DO? Blaise Pascal decided being wrong was a risk he could not take.

Blaise Pascal was your typical genius. He invented a mechanical calculator (this was 200 years before the first computer), proved vacuums could exist, and developed the field of probability, the math of chance. In later years, Pascal turned to theology and his writings were later published in a book called *Pensées* (meaning "thoughts"). One of his thoughts was about taking a wager on whether God does not exist. Betting against God and finding you were wrong would result in eternal damnation in hell. Betting for God and finding you were wrong would result in a finite loss—the denial of pleasures in life. Pascal said that meant we should always behave as if God existed.

A vision of hell is enough to make us behave in a religious way, according to Blaise Pascal. After all, what have you got to lose?

34 Spinoza's Ethics

Spinoza said that God is in everything—the clay of a pot, the body of the potter, and the eye of whoever sees the pleasing result.

BARUCH SPINOZA IS BEST REMEMBERED FOR HIS BOOK *ETHICS*, which in fact outlines how the Dutch philosopher didn't believe in doing the right thing. Instead, God was in charge of everything.

To Spinoza the human mind was incapable of understanding true reality, which was infinite in its perfection. This was an opposing view to the mind–body dualism of Descartes. Spinoza argued that the human need for emotion and good and bad was a response to our inability to see the biggest picture. In reality, the concepts of good and bad had no place in the amoral Universe.

In his book, Spinoza reasoned that if God were infinite, there could be no portion of the Universe that was not God. So what we term "nature"—planet Earth and all the rest—was the same as "God." We humans were part of God as well. (Many commentators suspect that Spinoza was an atheist and this was his way of saying it.) Nature is worthy of love, but does not offer any in return, nor does it judge, and the same is true of God, said Spinoza. As part of God, our lives were predetermined, and morality and free will were an illusion.

35 Locke: Human Understanding

ENGLISHMAN JOHN LOCKE WAS ONE OF THE FIRST EMPIRICISTS, a philosopher who believed that we are born a blank slate, and our minds and knowledge are the product of our experience.

John Locke began a long tradition among philosophers. He imagined a mind swap. What would happen if two people woke up one day with each other's memories? Their bodies would be unchanged as would their circumstances, but they would no longer remember how they had ended up in that particular bed in that house. The history of their body was unknown to them—they remember the history of another body, which is somewhere else. So, in the end, who are they?

NATURE VERSUS NURTURE

Which part of us is prefigured when we are born and what is the product of our experiences in life? This is that nature versus nurture debate, which continues to this day. Locke thought our minds are entirely the product of nurture, starting as a blank slate, or *tabula rasa*. However, he accepted we are born with innate abilities—to learn to speak, for example, or to sense our surroundings.

Tabula rasa

In his *Essay Concerning Human Understanding,* Locke suggested that the human mind or consciousness was a *tabula rasa* (meaning "cleaned tablet"). It was born empty of concepts and was shaped by acquiring a hierarchy of ideas, beginning with the most simple—light, dark, smooth, sharp, etc.—and gradually building up over a lifetime as the mind made sense of the world in which it found itself.

Many philosophers before him had asserted that at least some of the contents of the self were innate. Plato believed our souls knew everything; it is just we had forgotten it all at birth, and needed to jog our memories. Others suggested that God imprinted universal ideas (mostly about God) in everyone's minds. Locke refused to accept that any innate knowledge existed, and that the self was entirely plastic, changing in many ways as we grow up and reason ourselves into existence. Since the self is the contents of a mental record of life, if that is lost or changed, the self changes with it. If someone loses their memory completely—like our mind-swap pair—and can only rely on new experiences, do they become an entirely different person?

In the 1660s, Robert Hooke used a microscope—a new invention at the time—to see the cells in the tissues of plants and animals for the first time. The microscope enhanced our senses and revealed a new understanding of nature.

36 Existence and Perception

IN THE 18TH CENTURY, GEORGE BERKELEY THOUGHT IT WAS ALL IN YOUR HEAD.
To him the only things that existed were ideas and the minds that had them.

Berkeley's philosophy is sometimes summed up as "to be is to be perceived," although that fails to account for minds, which are doing the perceiving—including perceiving

themselves. Although this Anglo-Irish bishop did not doubt that the physical world was out there, he said that all we have are mental impressions of it—there is no evidence of anything else. And that means that the world does not cause us to understand it in a particular—or truthful—way. Instead we project our own experience onto it, and causes and effects we might observe are down to our actions, not those of nature itself.

Berkeley might have questioned whether this tree had fallen over, unless he had seen it do so. Whatever happens, he said, it is all in the mind.

37 Best of all Possible Worlds

AS THE CODISCOVERER OF CALCULUS ALONG WITH ISAAC NEWTON, GOTTFRIED LEIBNIZ was a clever fellow to be sure. However, he was happy to accept that the human mind was limited—but that was nothing to worry about.

Leibniz, a German diplomat by trade, had a different approach to Berkeley (one of the "British empiricists"). He was a rationalist and believed that he could think up knowledge and not be reliant on evidence from his experiences. However, he admitted the latter was an important source of understanding, due to the fact that the human mind was incapable of using reason alone to truly understand the whole of nature in all its infinite complexity. Only God was clever enough for that. So, we humans had to find things out through experience as well.

Leibniz divided knowledge arrived at by reason into "necessary" truths and "contingent" ones. The answer to a mathematical calculation is a necessary truth because it contains everything you need to know for it to be true, and so can never be untrue. Contingent truths are facts that may be correct at one time—you are reading page 47—but not all the time (once you've turned the page). Humans understand the Universe as a series of contingent truths, while God knows it all as necessary truths. So while we are moving through time, experiencing new things and learning truths from them, God has understood it all already using his divine reason. Since God is the epitome of goodness, the truths that he has figured out about the Universe are also purely good. Therefore, Leibniz suggests, we should be optimistic about the future because we live in the best of all possible worlds.

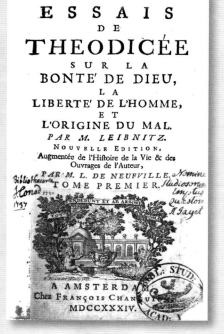

THE PRIORITY

Leibniz's optimistic outlook must have been tested when he became locked in a vitriolic argument with Isaac Newton over who had the priority over calculus—who got there first. Leibniz published in 1684, 20 years before Newton, although the Englishman's notes showed that he had developed the ideas decades earlier than his rival. The dispute produced a rift between English and continental scientists for decades. The outcome was the best possible for Leibniz in the end. Although Newton got there first, it is Leibniz's version of calculus that is taught today.

Leibniz set out much of his optimistic philosophy in the 1710 book Théodicée *(or Essays on the Goodness of God, the Freedom of Man, and the Origin of Evil).*

38 Voltaire's Skepticism

BEST REMEMBERED AS THE AUTHOR OF THE SATIRICAL NOVEL *CANDIDE*, VOLTAIRE WAS ONE OF THE ENLIGHTENMENT'S EARLY COMMENTATORS. While new truths were being revealed by various means, he remained skeptical.

By the 18th century, Europe's Age of Enlightenment was in full swing, with scientists and philosophers questioning every norm. This was the time when science was beginning to really change our understanding of the world, but Voltaire could not help but be skeptical about all the energetic paradigm-smashing.

In 1759, Voltaire personified the optimistic spirit of the Age of Enlightenment in the form of Dr. Pangloss, a relentlessly upbeat character in his satire Candide. *The inspiration behind the doctor was said to be Gottfried Leibniz.*

He felt that old certainties provided by religion and Scholasticism were being replaced by new ones, a fact that he found absurd. Scientists pronounced new discoveries as "fact," only to have them altered by later developments. He saw this readiness to accept certainties, old or new, as the easy way out, when the better path was to doubt the veracity of everything and to constantly challenge truth. With that in mind, he argued that rulers (the French king, for example) should have their powers limited. Soon after his death, the French Revolution attempted just that.

39 Hume: Rational Beliefs

DAVID HUME WAS THE TOWERING FIGURE OF BRITISH EMPIRICISM.
He refused to take any knowledge for granted, and so ended
up questioning even the most basic natural phenomena.

HUME'S FORK

David Hume divided truths into two groups
using a system now known as Hume's fork:
Demonstrative truths are true *a priori*—you do
not have to investigate to check their veracity,
but in the end tell you trivial facts. Probable
truths have to be verified *a posteri*—through
evidence—and may not always be true all the
time. If a statement fits neither one of these
groups, it cannot be true.

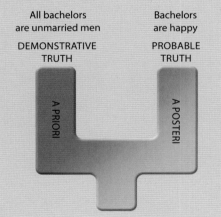

All bachelors are unmarried men	Bachelors are happy
DEMONSTRATIVE TRUTH	PROBABLE TRUTH
A PRIORI	A POSTERI

Scotsman Hume was heading in the same direction
as his English antecedents, the empiricists Locke
and Berkeley: There was no such thing as innate
knowledge in place prior to birth. Instead, all we can
ever know is learned through our experience. Then
Hume challenged the idea of knowledge further and
revealed that even the most primitive concepts about our
place in the world were neither true nor false.

Two forms of truth

To begin with Hume divided ideas into two groups. A thought
could be an "impression," a direct perception of the world
through the senses or an emotional response to it. If not an
impression, then the thought was an "idea," which in Hume's
terms was composed of many impressions, reflections of past
experiences that we combine into a novel concept or imagining.
Having divided up our minds in this way, Hume then pointed
out that our ideas do not always have the full backing of our
impressions. He explains by using another dichotomy, often
referred to now as Hume's fork (*see* box). A statement is either
demonstrative or probable. The best examples of demonstrative

Hume was an early starter, beginning his inquiry into truth at the age of 18, and setting out his famous philosophy before the age of 30.

The Sun always rises in the morning. However, Hume argued this was not true—one day it might not. Even these "regularities of nature" could not be relied on as being fact.

statements, in fact the only ones that Hume would really countenance, were mathematical equalities: 3+1 = 4, 4-2 = 2, etc. The truth of these statements is self-evident, even prior to experiencing or checking the veracity of the result. In other words the truth is *a priori* (before experience).

The second type of statement is probable: 400 apples are enough to fill a barrel. You can never know if this is true unless you put 400 apples into a barrel. And of course the figure of 400 would not be true for all barrels—some could hold more or fewer. Nevertheless, once the truth of the statement has been verified *a posteri*—after experience—then it is just as true as 2+2 = 4.

Not one nor the other

However, Hume then pointed out that many of the statements we make about the world are neither demonstrative nor probable truths. "The Sun will rise in the morning" is a good example. This is not demonstrative because there is nothing specific about the Sun that means it has to rise in the morning—it will still be the Sun if it does not. However, the Sun always rises in the morning: It has done so every day of your life—and Hume's life too. However, that does not make its rising a probable truth. It can only be such once we watch it rise and see the evidence for ourselves. The mistake we make is that we are so used to the cycle of sunrise and sunset and other natural patterns that we assume they will continue. We infer from the fact that the Sun has always risen in the morning that it will do so tomorrow morning, but we can never be certain that it will.

Hume extended this uncertainty to cause and effect. The idea that hitting a drum causes a sound is not demonstrative because there is no logical reason to say the sound has no other cause. And we cannot check every sound of every drumbeat to test it empirically. So there is no rational basis of cause and effect, just our human "custom" of using patterns to understand nature.

SCOTTISH ENLIGHTENMENT

David Hume was a leading figure in what is known as the Scottish Enlightenment. Eighteenth-century Scotland was a highly literate country, with three-quarters of people able to read and write—far more than many other countries. As a consequence, Scottish thinkers from this time had a far-reaching impact. They include Adam Smith, the founder of economics; Joseph Black, a chemist who investigated the nature of heat; and James Hutton, a geologist who developed the idea of uniformitarianism. This says that deeper rocks are older than shallow ones. One of his diagrams is shown below. Hutton's idea led people to reconsider the age of the Earth and inspired theories of evolution.

40 The Social Contract

EARLIER THINKERS HAD BLAMED HUMAN NATURE ON THE TROUBLES OF SOCIETY, BUT ONE FRENCH PHILOSOPHER SAW IT ANOTHER WAY. Jean-Jacques Rousseau wondered if it was society itself that created all the problems.

The European Enlightenment was all about questioning long-held truths. Scientists of the period were hailed as heroes of progress, given free rein to shatter our understanding of nature—and provide new technologies and commercial opportunities. However, philosophers were frequently in trouble. They were often forced into exile and censored as they sought to shake up the political status quo, questioning the power of the Church and aristocracy.

> *"Man is born free and everywhere he is in chains."*
>
> ROUSSEAU

Society corrupts

Jean-Jacques Rousseau was one such political philosopher following in the footsteps of the likes of Thomas Hobbes in discussing the tacit agreement, or contract, that people made with the state. Hobbes had taken a dim view of the natural state of humanity. He believed that people were only motivated by self-interest, with the result that society was created to protect individuals from each other. Rousseau took the polar opposite view. "Natural humans" who came before society were entirely innocent and free and, therefore, filled with an innate compassion for each other. Rousseau also went against accepted thinking by saying it was society, with its apparently high-minded culture, art, and science, that corrupted people, leading them to behave in selfish and destructive ways. In other words, being "civilized" meant being cruel, unhappy with life, and, above all, not free. However, Rousseau regarded society as an inevitable and necessary ill that results from humanity's ability to reason and impose its will on nature.

NATURAL NOBILITY

Rousseau's view of the natural human, or *bon sauvage* is often mistaken to mean "noble savage." The 18th century was a time of rapid colonial expansion, and Europeans were frequently encountering new cultures, which they characterized as savage—meaning "brutish"—but still dignified. However, Rousseau's phrase is mistranslated—it refers to a "natural goodness" of primitive humans before they were corrupted by society.

Living together

According to Rousseau it all began innocently enough, as people began to claim land and property for themselves, and laws were needed to protect ownership. However, the rules of society force people to lose sight of their natural characteristics and encourage them to behave selfishly. In the end, laws curtail freedom and make people miserable.

The solution according to Rousseau was set out in his 1762 book, the *Social Contract*. In it he argues that the state should not be run by a few aristocrats but by all members of society. Citizens should be allowed to live in their natural state—Rousseau imagined this to be some bucolic idyll, where people were mostly farmers and lived surrounded by nature—and together they would formulate the laws in what he called the "general will." To achieve a more natural state, education would be unnecessary—learning about the world only led to corruption. Rousseau also had similar things to say about the detrimental effects of religion on human beings' ability to live together in harmony.

Left to their own devices, the general will of the people would manifest naturally and "come from all and apply to all." The citizens would be free again. They would have no need to foster inequalities brought about by the desire for property, and a sense of belonging would appear among all members of society. Rousseau phrased this end state as "liberté, égalité, and fraternité," meaning "freedom, equality, and brotherhood." That phrase is the motto of the French Republic to this day.

An 1818 oil painting in the Romantic style by Caspar Friedrich, The Wanderer above the Sea of Fog, *sums up Rousseau's ideal view of humanity: Noble and free but unable to see clearly into the future.*

REVOLUTIONARY THINKING

Rousseau's writings were banned in France and he spent periods in exile to avoid the ire of the all-powerful French monarchy. The injustice and inequality of life in France were creating a great deal of discontent, and Rousseau's ideas were not short of supporters. In 1789, 11 years after his death, the French Revolution began with the storming of the Bastille fortress in Paris (right).

France had been beaten in several wars and had become a poor country, and French citizens felt aggrieved by the heavy taxation they were forced to pay to support King Louis XVI's luxurious lifestyle. Rousseau's opening statement to the *Social Contract*: "Man is born free, yet everywhere he is in chains," became a slogan during the ten years of conflict. However, despite his ideas being widely espoused by revolutionary leaders, the resultant French Republic was not the return to the natural state of humanity as advocated by Rousseau, but tyranny in another form.

41 Wealth of Nations

SELF-INTEREST NEED NOT BE A SOCIAL PROBLEM, SAID ADAM SMITH, THE SO-CALLED FATHER OF ECONOMICS IN 1776. THE THING THAT SETS HUMANITY APART FROM ANIMALS IS THAT WE MAKE bargains with each other, forming equitable agreements that appeal to the self-interest of both sides.

Adam Smith was not just a thinker, he was also in charge of overseeing imports to Britain.

"Man is an animal that makes bargains: No other animal does this—no dog exchanges bones with another." This sums up Adam Smith's central philosophical view of humanity, which underlies his economic theory. While Smith was happy to accept that people were capable of great altruism and compassion toward each other, he said you could not rely on that behavior. It was much more sensible to expect a person to act in their self-interest, and that would benefit everyone. To rely on people's goodwill alone to get what you need—food, clothing, housing, etc.—will fail, because as Smith puts it, producing all those things requires the cooperation of a "great multitude." This book, for example, required someone to write it, check the spellings, organize the pictures, design the pages, work the printing press, make the paper, grow the trees for wood

THE INVISIBLE HAND

Adam Smith described the law of supply and demand as an "invisible hand" that controlled the prices in a market. At the time the most advanced markets were in the Netherlands, where shares of goods being produced around the world were bought and sold (below). The invisible hand pushed up prices of goods that were scarce yet in demand, and pushed down prices of products that were abundant.

pulp... The list is surprisingly long. The way we all work together is by making bargains. Each bargain involves the exchange of labor or goods in return for money or some other benefit. Both sides agree to the bargain because they both gain from it. Smith summed it up this way: "The best way for you to get what you want is for you to give me what I want."

> *"No society can surely be flourishing and happy, of which the far greater part of the members are poor and miserable."*
>
> SMITH

Adam Smith's economic theory was presented in Wealth of Nations *in 1776, often regarded as one of the most influential books ever published.*

Commercial society

Smith argued that commerce and money benefit society in that each person is freed from being self-sufficient. We don't farm all of our food ourselves. Instead, we specialize in providing a single service in exchange for everything else. Smith went on to suggest that market forces could create a perfect society, where everyone is free to pursue their individual interests. Smith reasoned that we do not all want the same things out of life, and people would be able to bargain to meet their particular needs rather than compete to acquire a share of the same kinds of things.

Giving people the freedom to choose which bargains they make and, therefore, control over the progress of their lives was not the aim of Smith's philosophy. He said that this freedom was the means by which society could eradicate inequality for all. The laws of supply and demand would regulate production and price with great precision, and so allow everyone to successfully pursue and achieve their own self-interests, within the law of the land, of course. (Smith did not consider the possibility that many people might not have a clear idea of what they wanted to achieve and would just carry on pursuing more things in an attempt to find out.)

Smith's free-market economic theories are viewed by some with suspicion today, and no government anywhere has ever allowed the truly free markets he espoused—there are always some restrictions. However, when the ideas became public in the late 18th century, Smith was hailed as a revolutionary. His economics said that the basis of a nation's wealth was its working people, not its gold reserves, and so it was taken as a direct attack on the interests of the aristocracy.

MASS PRODUCTION

Adam Smith was very impressed with mass production. At the time, cotton mills and factories were springing up across Britain in what was to become the Industrial Revolution. Smith described how a "division of labor," in which workers specialized on one repetitive task, could boost productivity many times over. However, Smith saw the dehumanizing effect of reducing a worker to little more than a moving part in a production line, and suggested it should be regulated.

AN

INQUIRY

INTO THE

Nature and Caufes

OF THE

WEALTH OF NATIONS.

By ADAM SMITH, LL. D. and F. R. S.
Formerly Profeffor of Moral Philofophy in the Univerfity of GLASGOW.

IN TWO VOLUMES.

VOL. I.

LONDON:

PRINTED FOR W. STRAHAN; AND T. CADELL, IN THE STRAND.
MDCCLXXVI.

42 Critique of Pure Reason

IMMANUEL KANT WAS NOT STANDING FOR THE REPEATED ARGUMENTS THAT NOTHING EXISTED BUT THE MIND. Everyone knew there was an external physical world as well, and Kant used reason to prove it—almost.

Kant's most famous book is called the *Critique of Pure Reason* (published in 1781), in which he reconfigures the way we can understand our perceptions of the world. Many of his famous forebears, such as Descartes, Hume, and Berkeley, had declared that there was no evidence for the outside world at all. The only certainties were contained in our minds. However, no one really believed that the entire Universe was a figment of the imagination; it was simply they could find no evidence for its physical existence. Kant thought that this was a major failing of philosophy and found a way to show the Universe was actually there, or at least show it was there just as much as our minds were. This breakthrough was significant in that it allowed scientists, who were busy exploring the physical world, to claim that their discoveries had some basis in truth.

All in time

Kant's reasoning on the existence of the external world goes like this: For something to exist, it must exist in time—have a start and end point. However, we cannot fix a start and end point to our own minds, only know they exist right now, in this instant. Now that instant has passed, your mind that existed within it has also gone, and the mind that exists right now is different, filled with different thoughts—

Kant is the most famous son of the city of Königsberg, then the capital of Prussia, and now the Russian city of Kaliningrad. In Kant's day the city was dominated by this castle (it was bombed in 1944), and the philosopher never strayed more than a few miles from the city.

MORAL PHILOSOPHY

Immanuel Kant (right) is also famous for his moral philosophy. He said we should judge the morality of someone's actions not by what they do but why they do it. Someone who acts to help another because of an emotional response is not as moral, says Kant, as someone who goes against their intuitive urges to do what they know is right. Doing a good deed to dispel your own negative emotions about their plight (let's say you feel sorry someone has cut themselves) is self-serving. To do the same deed despite being repulsed by it—say, not liking blood—is truly altruistic and thus more moral. Harsh but fair.

and so the process continues. So for the mind to exist in the continuous series of instants that we call time, that time must be anchored in the changes of the external world. We only know time passes because things change around us. So we need the external world to prove our minds exist—which we already knew anyway, thanks to Descartes—and so the external world must exist as well!

Just knowing

Kant explained that our perceptions of the world required us to know some things in advance—*a priori*. We cannot perceive the external world without an innate knowledge of space—we know that space exists outside of us before we sense the things in it. The same is true of substance, says Kant. We require things to change through time before we are able to grasp our own existence and sense the external world. And for that we must have an innate concept of substance. Without it we are reduced to understanding the changes in the external world as distinct objects appearing for an instant and being replaced with other, slightly different ones. Instead, we understand that the properties of a single constant object are altering through time.

Two worlds

This position of innate knowledge made Kant an idealist in philosophical terms, but he amended that to "transcendental idealism" where the concepts of space and time and cause and effect belong to the *phenomenal* world, the world of our senses and mind. They are not a characteristic of the *noumenal* world, the name Kant gave to that which exists separately from our senses, sometimes called "things-in-themselves." The idea that reality must be approached as two distinct worlds puts some restrictions on what we as humans can ever know. We cannot ever see beyond the phenomenal world and look outside of space and time.

KANT'S TRIDENT

Immanual Kant's transcendental idealism reconfigured Hume's fork (*see* page 48) into what has been dubbed Kant's trident. Two of the prongs are more or less the same. Kant describes statements that are true by definition (*a priori*) as analytic knowledge, while statements that require evidence are synthetic. Analytic statements are trivial—they depend on the meaning of words. Synthetic statements tell us something about the world, which is true at that moment at least. Kant said it is possible for synthetic statements to be true *a priori* as well. To do this we use analytic knowledge to confirm a synthetic statement. That statement is *a priori* and so does not require evidence and is always true, but it is also synthetic because it reveals something non-trivial about reality.

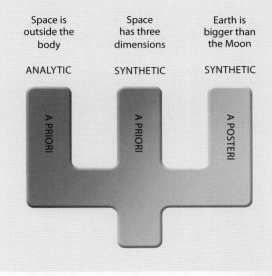

Space is outside the body	Space has three dimensions	Earth is bigger than the Moon
ANALYTIC	SYNTHETIC	SYNTHETIC
A PRIORI	A PRIORI	A POSTERI

43 Burke's Political Philosophy

EDMUND BURKE WAS A BRITISH POLITICIAN WHO SET OUT A VISION OF SOCIETY that still resonates in the ups and downs of modern political discourse.

Burke preferred gradual social change but supported the American Revolution as it was a fight against colonialism.

Burke was a politician in the last half of the 18th century, when the philosophies of Hobbes, Rousseau, Smith, and others were having a real impact on social development. British society was increasingly becoming commercialized and the concept of a social contract was accepted as fact. In return for obedience to the state and the paying of taxes, people expected some kind of representation and influence over the common good. Britain's American colonies were becoming increasingly unwilling to keep that agreement with the state run from London. Similar things were happening in France, albeit by different means, as the poor of France were growing discontented with the status quo of an absolute monarchy, a monarch who lived in luxury while they struggled for survival.

After the French Revolution came the Terror, in which many people were executed, This vindicated Burke's opposition to the overthrow of the traditional French state.

Slow but steady

Edmund Burke was not a revolutionary. He disagreed with Rousseau that the social contract could be broken at any time if enough people wanted it. He advocated that society was bound by its traditions, and could only make successful changes gradually. Radical changes were never a good idea, and as a result he opposed the French Revolution once it started. However, Burke was a supporter of the American struggle for independence, because its aims were less extensive. In the end, the American rebels were wanting to fulfill their rightful social contract, not to rip it up and start again as was happening in France.

Burke is often said to be the first political conservative. He advocated property ownership and free-market economics as a social good but defended traditions. However, at the center of his political philosophy,

"WHEN GOOD MEN ..."

The famous saying: "The only thing necessary for evil to triumph is for good men to do nothing" is often attributed to Edmund Burke, but we are not sure he ever said it. He did say something similar, although a lot less pithy: "When bad men combine, the good must associate; else they will fall, one by one, an unpitied sacrifice in a contemptible struggle."

Burke was interested in ensuring that all benefits of human endeavor, such as art and charity, not just the ones that had commercial value, were recognized by a social contract. It was not just the things that had a price that should be valued.

To that end he argued that society was not just an agreement between a group of people who had a common interest in the here and now. Instead, society had its roots in the traditions handed down by past generations.

Burke disagreed with John Locke that education was the key to a good society. Locke believed that everyone started life as a blank slate with the potential to learn anything and to be taught how to behave well. In contrast, Burke subscribed to original sin, where the wrongs of ancestors tainted the souls of the generations to come, and it was society's traditions and customs that guided people to live a moral life. In that respect, every generation had an obligation to enhance its customs so future generations could live yet more godly lives. This process could only occur gradually over many generations. "Things can only get better," might have been a good election slogan for him.

44 Utilitarianism

JEREMY BENTHAM'S PHILOSOPHY WAS SIMPLE. THE BEST THING TO DO WAS MAXIMIZE HAPPINESS. Everything should be judged by its utility, or usefulness, in making us feel good.

How can you live a happy life? Some might think that there is no simple answer, but in 1780 Jeremy Bentham had a go: Minimize pain and maximize pleasure. This was not a particularly new idea, but Bentham was interested in formalizing social reforms and he proposed a system of government that would make everyone happy, or at least as many people as possible. "The greatest happiness for the greatest number is the measure of right or wrong," he explained. In practical terms, when legislators are weighing up a change to the law, they should consider its utility, or effectiveness, in making people happy. If it is not possible to make everyone a bit happier, then the new law should be made to make at least a majority of people happier, even if that means condemning the rest of society to a reduction in happiness. Bentham's utilitarianism would go on to be the basis of great social reforms in the 19th century.

Englishman Jeremy Bentham was not buried after death. Instead, his body was embalmed and put on display at London University. It was Bentham's idea; he called it his auto-icon. (The head is actually made of wax—the real thing is too fragile to display.)

45 Feminism

MARY WOLLSTONECRAFT IS SAID TO BE THE FIRST FEMINIST. In the 18th century, she was challenging the dominance of men as far back, with arguments that are still being made today.

Looking back through history, there has never been a time when society was not ruled by men, for men, with women having to do what they were told. There have been inspirational women, warriors like Boudicca of ancient Britain, intellectuals like Hypatia of Alexandria, and powerful rulers like Catherine the Great of Russia. However, these figures were exceptional, taking their place in history under the auspices of male mentors or facilitators. There was no hint that women in general were the equal of men.

In the 1790s, Mary Wollstonecraft—teacher, novelist, and philosopher—stepped into this void. In the decade before, Wollstonecraft had set up a school near London where she educated boys and girls equally.

Wollstonecraft had a short, unhappy life, growing up in a violent household, unlucky in love and eventually dying in childbirth. The child, a girl, grew up to be Mary Shelley, the author of Frankenstein.

Denial of education

Wollstonecraft went on to be a powerful political writer, first championing republicanism as opposed to hereditary monarchy before focusing on the position of women in society. She rebutted the argument frequently leveled that women lacked

In the 18th century, gender roles were very restrictive. Men did most of the heavy physical labor, and were the public face of the family, while women had domestic roles and had no rights to property or public positions.

the mental capacities of men by suggesting women were systematically denied the same level of education.

As such, she drew on the ideas of John Locke and others, who proposed that the human mind is born empty, and its contents arrive through experience. Wollstonecraft argued that at birth, the female mind is just the same as a male one, and the differences seen between men and women at large are the products of differing levels of education. Her proposal was that women have the same right to an education as men. Instead of being chattels to be traded through marriage or confined to domestic work, Wollstonecraft wanted women to be equals to men, for husband and wife to be companions rather than master and servant. This simple idea struck at the very core of social traditions, and is still being debated today.

A VINDICATION OF THE RIGHTS OF WOMEN

Mary Wollstonecraft wrote this, her most famous book (ironically she wrote *Vindications of the Rights of Men* first in 1790), partly in response to the assertions of Jean-Jacques Rousseau. He had said that boys and girls should be educated differently, with the emphasis of female education being how to defer to men. It seems Rousseau's "natural human" was a bit of a sexist. Wollstonecraft's book did not find many fans at first, but became the cornerstone for the 20th-century feminist movement.

46 Philosophy of Philosophy

IN 1798, FRIEDRICH SCHLEGEL CALLED FOR A TIME-OUT. HE HAD A FEELING THAT PHILOSOPHY WAS GETTING CARRIED AWAY WITH ITSELF. In so doing, Schlegel heralded the Romantic Age where emotion was elevated above reason.

Schlegel, a German scholar, was as much poet and social commentator as he was philosopher. His work is indeed poetic, so much so it is often hard to figure out. However, as the 18th century drew to a close, Schlegel wondered what the Enlightenment philosophers had actually achieved. His philosophy of philosophy (metaphilosophy) makes the point that despite banging on about first principles, philosophers always start somewhere in the middle of a problem, inspired (or uninspired) by the work of others. Linear reasoning did not impress the decorative Shlegel: Philosophy, he said, "starts in the middle. It is a whole, and the path to recognizing it is no straight line, but a circle." Although it is not entirely clear what he meant, Schlegel changed the way we looked at philosophy from then on.

"Reason is mechanical, wit chemical, and genius organic spirit."

SCHLEGEL

47 Hegel's Spirit

PERHAPS THE MOST IMPORTANT PHILOSOPHER OF THE ROMANTIC PERIOD, GEORG HEGEL COMMUNICATED IN RIDDLES. Those who deciphered them found a new way of understanding human endeavors.

Hegel wrote much of his work in mysterious, enigmatic aphorisms, making his points more obscure than they needed to be. However, at their most basic, Hegel's ideas gave a new outlook on the phenomenal world as described by Kant—the world as experienced through our senses and minds. In his 1807 book, the *Phenomenology of Spirit*, Hegel says that every phenomenon, everything we perceive in the phenomenal world, is a manifestation of *Geist*, German for "spirit."

The story of human progress has been underwritten by the different fragments of the Spirit combining with each other. That is how philosophies, religions, political systems, science, and technology are always changing and improving as old ideas merge into a new one. Hegel was living in interesting times, when revolutions and reforms were transforming society at a fast pace. At the end of history, the Spirit will be whole again like a giant jigsaw, he said. In the meantime we are born into the ongoing process, where each generation inherits a new "Spirit of the Age" from the one before.

While Hegel was developing his philosophy, Napoleon conquered Prussia. He is seen here entering Berlin and Hegel watched him parade through his home city of Jena. Perhaps wisely Hegel characterized his new emperor as the embodiment of the zeitgeist, *or "spirit of the age."*

Hegel's Spirit reintegrates by a process called the dialectic (*see* box), which produces a new idea, or synthesis, from older conflicting ones—the thesis and antithesis. Hegel pointed out that one generation's synthesis can become the next one's thesis—another problem that needs solving. And so the Spirit continues to merge, heading inexorably toward a time when humanity understands everything!

THE DIALECTIC

Hegel's Spirit progressed through a process called the dialectic, where contradictory ideas—thesis and antithesis—were reconciled into a synthesis. An example would be tyranny and its opposite, anarchy. These combine to create law, which applies limits to both despotic rulers and the freedom of individuals.

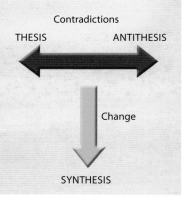

48 Laplace's Demon

THE FRENCH MATHEMATICIAN PIERRE-SIMON LAPLACE HAD ONE OF THE BIGGEST INTELLECTS IN HISTORY. However, even he did not know everything, but he wondered about the consequences of something that did.

Laplace was not one for the supernatural. In a famous exchange, the French emperor Napoleon Bonaparte, who was both his ruler and student, asked why there was no mention of a creator in his analysis of the motion of heavenly bodies. "I have no need of the hypothesis," replied Laplace, rather bravely—Napoleon was a despot, after all.

However, in 1814, Laplace did require a supernatural intelligence for a thought experiment into the nature of cause and effect and free will. The concept is known as Laplace's demon, although there is no suggestion that the intelligence was malevolent—the term demon simply evokes a ghostly being from outside of our current reality. Here is the idea in Laplace's own words: "We may regard the present state of the Universe as the effect of its past and the cause of its future. An intellect which at a certain moment would know all forces that set nature in motion, and all positions of all items of which nature is composed; if this intellect were also vast enough to submit these data to analysis, it would embrace in a single formula the movements of the greatest bodies of the Universe and those of the tiniest atom; for such an intellect nothing would be uncertain, and the future just like the past would be present before its eyes."

In other words, if it were possible to quantify the motion and behavior of every particle in the Universe, it would then be possible to predict how they would be interacting at every moment in the future. Without needing to create the Universe, the demon would, nevertheless, become omniscient, all-knowing. And as Boëthius had pointed out, such an intellect would deprive us of our free will. Laplace's idea is known as "scientific determinism," where the physical laws of nature underwrite every facet of the Universe, including the mind and will.

> *"What we know is not much. What we do not know is immense."*
>
> LAPLACE

The demon's great intellect would ensure the course of our lives was set in stone from start to finish.

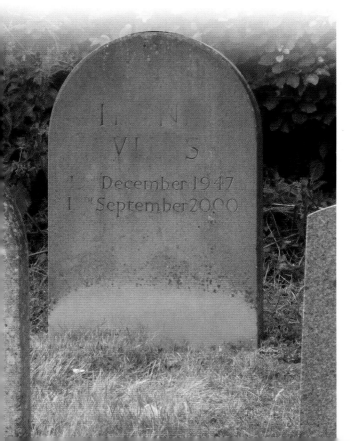

UNCERTAINTY PRINCIPLE

In the 1920s, the pioneers of quantum physics, Max Born and Werner Heisenberg, found that chance was a component in the behaviors of the smallest particles of nature. This became the Uncertainty Principle, which states that it is impossible to know both the location and motion of a particle at the same time. If you know one of them, the other can only be expressed in terms of probabilities. Therefore, as far as we know today, it is not possible to predict an effect arising from a cause at the quantum level. Laplace's demon would never be able to figure it all out in advance—unless he or she knows something we don't.

49 Schopenhauer's Vision

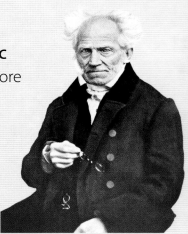

ARTHUR SCHOPENHAUER WAS NOT IMPRESSED WITH HEGEL'S OPTIMISTIC VIEW OF THE FUTURE OF HUMANITY. Instead, he envisioned a much more pessimistic future as humanity drifts through an uncaring Universe.

While he opposed the work of the Swabian Hegel (from southern Germany), Schopenhauer looked a lot more fondly on the writings of Kant, a fellow Prussian (from the northeast). Kant said that reality was in two unconnected realms, an external world (noumenal) and the world of ideas (phenomenal). In 1818, Shlegel agreed with the dichotomy but preferred to think of them as being two aspects of the same thing.

Schopenhauer pointed out that a person's knowledge was limited by the scope of their senses: "Every man takes the limits of his own field of vision to be the limits of the world." This allowed him to reinterpret the two aspects of reality as Will and Representation. Every object, most notably ourselves, has Will. Will is only perceived from within objects. Representation is what we can perceive outside our body. So we think about clapping our hands— that is the Will in action—and we perceive the hands moving together and making a noise—that is Representation.

This internal and external existence applies to all things, but we are aware only of our inner world, never that of other objects. However, since space and time are products of Representations, the Will is timeless and everywhere— and that means the same single Will fills you, me, and the entire Universe. But that is nothing to be glad about, said Schopenhauer. The universal Will has no benevolence and is directionless, leaving humans to find their own happiness—and frequently fail.

Not looking like much of a funster, Arthur Schopenhauer was largely ignored by his contemporaries. Only later was he an influence on such towering figures as Nietzsche and Freud.

EASTERN INFLUENCES

Schopenhauer's view of a universal Will that connects all things is an echo of Eastern philosophies, such as those linked to Hinduism and Buddhism. Schopenhauer was a scholar of Hindu scriptures, and his advice on how to live also rings true with the Buddha's suggestions, if tinged with a Germanic bluntness. The Will has no moral goal and the pursuit of pleasure is a transient escape resulting in inevitable suffering later down the line. The only way out is to give up the need for pleasure. Only if we realize our true state, as fragments of a single Will existing in an illusory Universe, can we begin to feel genuine empathy for each other.

50 Existentialism

SØREN KIERKEGAARD DEVELOPED A PHILOSOPHY COMPLETELY AT ODDS WITH THE INTERCONNECTED REALITY OF MORE ROMANTIC THINKERS. The Dane felt alone and suggested that was because he was—utterly.

In their own ways, thinkers of the Romantic Age cast humanity into grand universal schemes where people were infinitesimal entities against the broadest sweep of reality. In 1807, Hegel said people were the mere agents of history, while in the 1840s Schopenhauer was sure our minds were dots of consciousness drifting in an aimless Universe. Kierkegaard thought the human condition was a much simpler and much starker affair.

DIZZINESS OF FREEDOM

In his book, *The Concept of Anxiety*, published in 1844, Kierkegaard invites us to imagine that we are standing on the edge of a cliff. Looking over the edge is frightening and composed of two sources of fear: A fear of falling (and landing), and the fear of being free to jump over the edge. Kierkegaard called this second anxiety the "dizziness of freedom." Being anxious causes unhappiness but also rouses us from frivolous and reckless behaviors, and forces us to be sensible.

A determined self

Kierkegaard was prone to depression and his philosophy was in part a self-examination that he sought to generalize into an understanding of the human condition. Being human is all about choices, he said. We live or die by how we decide to behave, in a very real sense in how we confront the physical dangers and obstacles that cross our paths. However, humanity also relates to moral decisions, as we choose between living for pleasure alone or according to a system of ethics. So far, this is nothing new, you might say. However, Kierkegaard believed that each choice we make is ours alone, free of influence from our education or social traditions—if we choose it to be. And crucially, morality in this context is entirely subjective—even the difference between good and bad is up to us to decide.

Kierkegaard said that the same fear that drives our survival is present when we are making moral choices, a "dizziness of freedom" (*see* box, above), which can lead to anxiety and depression (certainly in his case).

Kierkegaard never called his philosophy existentialism but he is said to be the founding figure of this school of thought, which focuses on how we tackle the big questions of existence.

Jumping is always a possibility. Kierkegaard suggested all our fears arise from the responsibility of having to choose how to live—or die. This guy is perhaps less anxious than most, though. He's brought a parachute.

51 Evolution by Natural Selection

Right: A cartoon from 1874 derides Darwin's theory in a souvenir edition of a London newspaper. It is said that Darwin himself bought a copy!

THERE ARE MANY LABELS GIVEN TO THIS CONTROVERSIAL IDEA— HERESY, THEORY, FACT, EVEN RELIGION. However, it fits well with being a philosophy, providing an answer to the question: "Where did we come from?"

For most of recorded history, philosophy has been frequently wrapped up in theological problems, with divine beings always part of the final thesis. During the Enlightenment, people began to question religion, especially its role as a social institution but also its impact on how we understood morality. Few people of this time would have admitted to being an atheist, but it is widely believed that Bentham, Spinoza, Hume, Laplace, and other Enlightenment figures probably were. Charles Darwin, the lead author of the theory of natural selection, was not an atheist, but his work has been championed by atheists ever since, as proof that the complexities of nature could arise without the need for a designer— without God. However, Darwin, although perhaps not a traditional Christian himself, would have argued, as others have since, that his

THE LONDON SKETCH BOOK.

PROF. DARWIN.

This is the ape of form.
Love's Labor Lost, act 5, scene 2.
Some four or five descents since.
All's Well that Ends Well, act 3, sc. 7.

VOYAGE OF THE BEAGLE

Charles Darwin went to university in Cambridge with the intention of becoming an Anglican vicar. However, he was caught by the wildlife bug, almost literally: He spent his free time collecting beetles and other insects in the fields near the city. Before being ordained as a clergyman, Darwin wanted to see the world and in 1831, he got a place aboard HMS *Beagle*, a British warship tasked with surveying South America and the Pacific. It is often said he was the ship's naturalist, the 19th-century equivalent of Mr. Spock, the *Star Trek* science officer. However, Darwin was a paying passenger on the ship, looking for adventure. The voyage took five years, during which Darwin's world view was changed for good. He came back with the beginnings of an idea that would change the world.

ideas were merely a response to the "fixed laws" that control the Universe, and do not hope to comment on how that Universe and laws came into being.

Origin of our species

Darwin published his famous book on natural selection, *On the Origin of the Species*, in 1859, spurred into action after decades of doubt by news that Alfred Russel Wallace was about to announce the same idea independently. The shock wave from the book has been rising and falling ever since. Its most emotive point was to say that humans were nothing particularly special. We had arrived on the planet by precisely the same means as every other life form, from mushroom to monkey.

Darwin was a retiring character and seldom defended himself in public. Thomas Huxley, known as Darwin's bulldog, did the talking for him. A famous debate involving Huxley sums up the initial response to the theory of natural selection. The Bishop of Winchester asked whether Huxley was related to monkeys on his grandmother's or grandfather's side. This idea of a linear transformation of one animal into another is a frequent problem in discussions of evolution. It is a bit more complicated than that—but not much.

Natural selection

There are a few features of life that alerted Darwin to formulate his theory of natural selection: Firstly, animals (or any form of life) compete with each other for survival—to stay alive long enough to reproduce. Secondly, members of a population are not all identical: There is always some variation, and some members are better suited to survival than others. Darwin termed this "fitness." Therefore, in each generation the fittest individuals survive, while the least fit die. The fit ones have been "selected" from the starting group, and their offspring will form the next generation. This generation will be different from the one before, because the least fit individuals are no longer represented. However, there are still some that are fitter than others, so natural selection is still at work.

What constitutes fitness is not fixed. Habitats change, and so animals that once flourished may start to struggle, and natural selection alters the population with only the fittest surviving. Across the generations this results in minor tweaks to the species' characteristics, but in Darwin's time strong evidence was emerging that Earth was incredibly ancient, hundreds if not thousands of millions of years old. Darwin's suggestion was that over all this great length of time, a myriad tiny tweaks were enough to produce the wealth of life that covers the planet today—plus all the species that have become extinct. And they did so without the need for a guiding intelligence.

GETTING THE BILL

The finches of the Galápagos Islands in the Pacific are named for Darwin and often used as an example of natural selection in action. Isolated on the remote islands, several species of bird evolved from a single seed-eating ancestor, each one adapted to exploit different sources of food, as indicated by the varying bill shapes.

Nuts

Seeds

Grubs

Insects

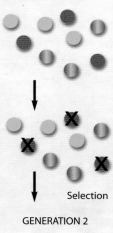

GENERATION 1

Selection

GENERATION 2

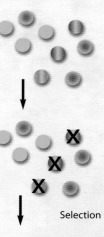

Selection

GENERATION 3

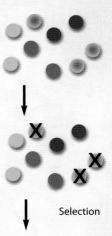

Selection

GENERATION 4

52 On Liberty

JOHN STUART MILL CREATED THE MODERN WORLD, BY DESCRIBING A SOCIETY THAT MOST OF US ARE HAPPY TO LIVE IN TODAY. And somewhat amazingly, this most influential of philosophers was something of a philosophical experiment himself.

John Locke had said that education and experience were the only influences on the contents of a person's mind, and John Stuart Mill's father decided to try that out—on baby John. Schooled at home using the Socratic Method to encourage critical thinking, young John turned out very well. At the age of eight he had mastered ancient Greek and was reading the classical philosophers in their own language. By 12 he was an expert in most things, except perhaps being a 12-year-old, and in his 20s he was easily holding his own among the finest minds of his generation.

Some say there was no finer philosopher in the 19th century than John Stuart Mill. He was without doubt a prodigious genius, but the question posed by Locke of the power of education still remained an open one. However, Mill's own philosophy was a more practical attempt to put it into action.

CHILD LABOR AND EDUCATION

Mill's philosophy had a transforming effect on Victorian Britain, which was a harsh place to live. Mill promoted education of children, saying that it would benefit not just them as individuals but also society as a whole. By the 1800s, Britain had become the first industrial society where children, some less than eight, were a large part of the workforce. In 1870, a new law was enacted to provide schooling (and prevent work) for every child until the age of 13. Mill did not focus that much on the working conditions in the new industrial society, but Karl Marx did (*see* page 68.)

Simply a pleasure

The Mills were family friends of Jeremy Bentham, and young John was tutored by the great man. In later life, Mill sought to clarify Bentham's ideas on utilitarianism. His main objection to them was Bentham's focus on using legislation to maximize the common good. Mill was not convinced that was a practical system at all. Surely such a blunt instrument as law would cause a great deal of unhappiness in some, as it promoted happiness in others. Also Bentham specifically chose not to judge one pleasure over another. However, Mill disagreed. He said it was better to be a discontented Socrates than

a happy fool. In Mill's view, once you had been exposed to the "higher" pleasures of literature, art, and music, you were never going to be as content with the more basic forms of fun. (His upbringing did make him a bit socially awkward, without much concept of the lives of ordinary folk.)

Nineteenth-century society was certainly ready for Mill's philosophy. Around the same time as the publication of On Liberty, *the Peabody Trust was set up by an American philanthropist to provide housing for the poor of London—as Mill would have said, providing "space to grow."*

Do no harm

That sounds rather paternalistic, but Mills was not going to be prescriptive. In his seminal work of 1859, *On Liberty*, Mills advocated education for the young, and proper housing to minimize restrictions on people reaching their fullest potential. However, once you were an adult, Mills said it was up to you. You were allowed to seek pleasure anyway you wanted, and the state would only step in if you were harming others.

Called the Harm Principal, this sounds entirely reasonable from a modern viewpoint, but at the time there was a sense in Victorian Britain that the state had a moral duty to keep the populous on a righteous path. However, Mill said

that being forced to live in accordance with the will of the majority, no matter how great, was the same as living under a tyranny imposed by a single, all-powerful despot.

Critics argued that Mill's idea would lead to a breakdown in morals, but he maintained it was the best way of achieving Bentham's goal of maximum happiness. Instead of the state acting to make people happy as Bentham had suggested, it should only act to stop one person making others unhappy. Mill was of the opinion that gradually, as education spread, society would elevate itself to pursue the higher pleasures. Modern societies are still heavily influenced by Mill's philosophy. Was he right?

The caption for this rather unkind caricature of John Stuart Mill in the British Vanity Fair *magazine from 1874 read: "A feminine philosopher."*

53 Marxism

KARL MARX WAS ANOTHER PHILOSOPHER WHO CERTAINLY LEFT A MARK ON HISTORY. WHILE HIS *COMMUNIST MANIFESTO* WAS LARGELY ignored when published in the 19th century, it became the basis of government for a third of the world during much of the 20th.

Karl Marx had a hard life even though he was not used to hard, physical labor. He wrote for a living, but was never able to earn much money.

Growing up in Germany, struggling to make ends meet, Karl Marx was unimpressed with the way life was turning out for him, and most of the people he saw around him. In his opinion, Adam Smith's warning about the dehumanizing effects of the free market had come to pass. As the economy had globalized during the age of empires, Smith's division of labor had spread at lightning speed. In industrialized societies individuals became more and more specialized in the manufacture of goods. In the end, Marx suggested (an end that was coming up fast upon us) that working people would become no more than particular moving parts in the great machinery of factories and mills. Such working people were valued only for the labor they could provide. Without property of their own, labor was the only thing they had left to sell to survive.

Divided society

This sorry state of affairs was down to an unequal split in society between the working class, or proletariat, and the capital-owning class, the bourgeoisie. This second group had arisen from the preindustrial society, where most people had existed as farmers and craftsmen. In the early 19th century, that work had been industrialized and the "means of production"—the factory machinery and production lines—were in the hands of the few, the bourgeoisie. Marx had a famous solution to this iniquity: The workers must control the means of production.

Recent history had shown Marx that social reforms occurred through revolution. His political thinking was formed before John Stuart Mill had proposed a means by which society could be improved by gradual change. Instead, Marx had been inspired by another: Georg Hegel.

REVOLUTIONS OF 1848

The year 1848 was one of revolutions. France, Germany, Poland, Italy, even Brazil all experienced popular uprisings, mostly ending in a brutal backlash by government forces. The *Communist Manifesto* of Marx and Friedrich Engels was published just before these tumultuous events, and while not inspiring them, certainly captured the mood of many in Europe. However, the failure of the revolutions resulted in a generation of disillusionment in political philosophy.

THE BOURGEOISIE

The word *bourgeoisie* was not invented by Marx. It is derived from the French word *burgeis*, which refers to a merchant or urban tradesman. In the Marxist context it is a person of property, who lived well at the expense of the poor. Marx assumed the revolution would occur in industrial societies with a large bourgeoisie. In fact, only agrarian states had communist revolutions.

The dialectic

Hegel's method for explaining the progress of history was called the dialectic, where conflicts between a thesis and an antithesis were resolved by a synthesis. Hegel had meant this to refer to the spiritual aspects of humanity, which contribute to the development of human nature. Marx saw it as a way of understanding actual historical events, such as revolutions—including what he saw as the inevitable communist revolution to come. He predicted that once all property was in the hands of the bourgeoisie—to him Britain was the closest society to this condition—then the synthesis would be a workers' rebellion where they would wrest control of all capital and create a perfect society free of Heglian conflicts. Marx said this revolution would be different to any others. Previous ones had been led by middle-class, even bourgeois, revolutionaries who carried popular support. In the communist revolt, the revolutionaries would be the workers themselves.

Communist Manifesto

Marx had set out this theory in the *Communist Manifesto* in collaboration with fellow German, Friedrich Engels (who also supported him financially). The short pamphlet was like no other philosophy—its aim was not to simply interpret the world but to change it. The document was published in 1848 under the auspices of the Communist League, a London-based political group dominated by German exiles. After a decade of living abroad, Marx returned to Germany in 1848 to support the revolt that was happening there (not quite a workers' revolution, but it was better than nothing). When that failed, he returned to London and lived the next 35 years in poverty. In that time he wrote the first volume of *Das Kapital*, published in 1867, an analysis of capitalism with the aim of eradicating it.

The October Revolution of 1917 in Russia was the first opportunity to put Marxism to the test in what became the Soviet Union led by Vladimir Lenin. The result was decades of oppression before an economic collapse precipitated reforms that led to the end of the Soviet Union in 1991.

54 Intentionality

BY 1874, THE PHYSICAL AND MENTAL WORLDS HAD been described in great detail, but they were still regarded as being made of substances.

Physical substance had heft and form, while mental substance was weightless and diffuse, but both were made of a "thing." German philosopher Franz Brentano swept away the need for this interpretation. The only feature that differentiated the worlds was "intentionality." The mental world had it—ideas always refer to something—while the physical world did not. It just is. This block of paper, board, ink, and glue in your hands has no intentionality. However, when you read it, the ideas in your head do. To Brentano, even something as visceral and "thoughtless" as pain had intentionality—it's intention is to warn you about damage to the body.

55 Man and Superman

IF SØREN KIERKEGAARD DISCOVERED EXISTENTIAL ANGST, FRIEDRICH NIETZSCHE found existential rage. His writings were eclectic yet bold and heralded an era of extremes, where humanity explored the limits of right or wrong.

Brilliant and eccentric in equal measure, Nietzsche got our attention with a very powerful statement in his most famous book, *Thus Spake Zarathustra*: God is dead! That is a strange thing to imagine. How can an omnipotent and infinite being ever die? Well, Nietzsche was an atheist and of the opinion that God never existed, but that was not the full meaning of his oft-quoted slogan. Instead, he was making the point that morality was anchored in the concept of God, a benevolent but judgmental being who could see everything we do. Nietzsche did not believe morality needed to be like this. In fact, he turned the whole thing on its head. Where Christianity (and other world religions) put insulting God as the highest blasphemy, Nietzsche said that to stay in awe of God was blasphemy against life! Plato had said the true world was beyond our senses in the world of Forms, and similarly, Christian teaching said that the true, higher world of heaven lay beyond death. For Nietzsche, it was all about the here and now.

Even in a sympathetic portrait, the pathological zeal that drove Nietzsche insane shines through.

Heroes and slaves

As a leading figure in the rather amorphous philosophical tradition known as existentialism, Nietzsche believed that morality, the difference between good and bad, was a subjective choice made by each one of us. The idea that God gave us morality was just a human-made tradition. Instead, he said that our morality lay in the myths of

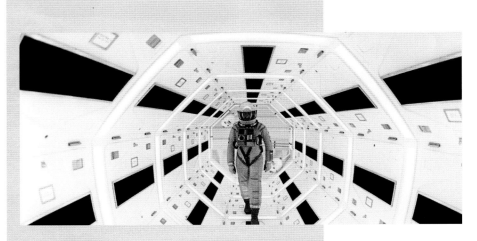

THUS SPAKE ZARATHUSTRA

The iconic sound track of the cult 1968 movie, *2001: Space Odyssey*, shares the title of Nietzsche's book. The music was written in 1896 by Richard Strauss who was inspired by the work. The film is about Dave, an astronaut who travels into space to investigate aliens. After the onboard computer "slave" makes a failed attempt to become the "master," Dave makes a leap to a new level of human, or superhuman, consciousness.

ancient times, such as those of Greece, where heroes triumphed through power and nobility. In response, the mortal humans developed a "slave morality," where strength and dominance were bad, while helping the weak and needy was good. Nietzsche advocated casting away our slave morality and returning to the more heroic "master morality," seizing the opportunity to be everything we could be—and more. He proposed that people who "revalued their values" and lived by a master morality would drive humanity to new heights. Such a person would be an Übermensch (above human, or more popularly, a superman).

It is not uncommon for people who can think so differently from the rest of us to suffer periods of mental illness. Nietzsche was one of them and spent his later years in an asylum. Control of his work went to his sister Elisabeth. She was an anti-Semite and nationalist and edited her brother's work to reflect her views. As a result Friedrich's name became an inspiration for Nazism, totally at odds with the jolly, life-affirming philosophy he espoused.

Nietzsche's philosophy swept away any limits on what humanity was allowed to do—anything was possible. However, he was opposed to nationalism and would not have thought that Nazis were supermen.

56 Pragmatism

AFTER A CENTURY OF ROMANTIC PHILOSOPHY, CONCERNED WITH SPIRITS, HEROES, AND GREAT EVENTS, William James developed a new tradition: Philosophy that was meant to be effective—but was it true?

An eminent American academic at the turn of the 20th century, William James began his journey into pragmatism because of a squirrel—or so the story goes. He was asked to solve a problem imagined by some colleagues. A hunter is looking for a squirrel on a tree trunk, but the squirrel is not about to get caught that easily. As the hunter circles the trunk, the squirrel scuttles around the other side, always staying just out of view. The question was, is the hunter circling the squirrel?

James's answer was yes and no. If by "circling" one meant moving around the squirrel in reference to the Earth—i.e. moving to the north, east, south, and west of the rodent—then yes, the hunter was circling. If the term "circling" referred to orientations with respect to the squirrel (behind, in front, etc.), then no, the hunter was not circling: He or she remained face to face with the prey at all times (although the tree was in the way).

While James was promoting his version of philosophical pragmatism in the early 1900s, U.S. President Theodore Roosevelt was forging ahead with a political pragmatism, as shown in this 1905 cartoon entitled "One of Mr Roosevelt's Quiet Days." Both approaches are open to question.

True value

Then James asked the question that we were all thinking: "What difference does it make?" As a pragmatist philosopher, the true answer was the one that had a benefit in understanding your proposition. In this case, neither of the answers were true because they gave no insight.

A pragmatic approach is consistent with objective facts. It is true to say stone is hard because that is useful to know (especially for those of us in glass houses). However, it can also be applied to subjective beliefs. Does God exist? James said yes because it was more useful to think that. His argument was similar to Pascal's Wager and the Ontological Argument: Once you've thought of God, it is more useful to believe in him. But that kind of thinking leaves pragmatism open to the claim that it treats truth as different from fact. Perhaps we should ask Santa Claus what he thinks the next time we see him?

> *"Every way of classifying a thing is but a way of handling it for some particular purpose."*
>
> JAMES

He attends to Santo Domingo | He hands Mr. Castro a few | He jumps on the Senate

He writes on the race question | He lands on Standard Oil | He attends a banquet

He superintends the preparations for inauguration day | He passes a hot message to the Senate | He pauses a moment to make plans for a hunting trip

ONE OF MR. ROOSEVELT'S QUIET DAYS

57 Philosophy of Language

IN THE 1900S, THE WORK OF SWISS PHILOSOPHER FERDINAND DE SAUSSURE LAID THE FOUNDATIONS OF SEMIOTICS, A FIELD THAT BREAKS DOWN LANGUAGE to its most basic components, common to every spoken tongue.

The starting point of semiotics is that language is not a simple link between sound and objects or concepts. Instead, it is made up of units called "signs." Every sign has two parts. The first is the "signifier," best described as its "sound image." This is the mental image associated with the sound of the word. In the vast majority of cases, the sound has no particular link to the image. The second part is the "signified," which is the broader meaning of the sign which depends on the other signs used in the phrase.

58 Learning from the Past

IN 1905, GEORGE SANTAYANA SAID, "THOSE WHO CANNOT REMEMBER THE PAST ARE CONDEMNED TO REPEAT IT." He was not offering a warning to future generations, but attempting to explain how knowledge develops.

The Spanish American's aphorism is frequently repurposed into "Those who do not remember the past..." and is used to suggest that we are at risk of making the same disastrous mistakes as our ancestors if we do not learn where they went wrong. That is true enough, but Santayana was trying to get a bit deeper. His was a naturalistic philosophy, the gist of which was that knowledge and the human condition have been accumulated over the years. They were not changed by great events but gradually morphed as each new generation contemplated the history of those who went before and made the necessary changes to adapt to the current conditions. In this way, human civilization does not discard the mistakes of the past but uses them to create the successes of the future.

The Trojan Horse is a famous lesson from history. Should we still "fear Greeks bearing gifts"?

59 How We Think

IN 1910, JAMES DEWEY PUBLISHED *HOW WE THINK*, A BOOK THAT RETARGETED PHILOSOPHY. Despite what we might want to believe, philosophy is entirely a practical pursuit.

Dewey was a member of the American pragmatism school. As such he believed that philosophy was not about exploring esoteric conundrums that have little bearing on life. Instead, it should focus on solving tangible problems that would make life easier. That is how philosophy began. Dewey disapproved of philosophers as spectators; instead, he

wanted them to be constantly evaluating the problems of each generation, assessing the efficacy of any ideas to solve them. In this way, truth was not a fixed concept, but something that everyone could agree was the best fit for the problem at hand.

Think about this problem. What's the best way to solve it?

60 Psychoanalysis

THE STUDY OF MENTAL ILLNESS IS ONE OF THE AREAS WHERE PHILOSOPHY AND SCIENCE MERGE. PSYCHOANALYSIS IS AN ATTEMPT TO bring a medical approach to the hopes and fears that populate our minds.

If the saying, "Physician heal thyself" is valid, then so must be "Philosopher know thyself." Sigmund Freud tried to live by both these concepts as he delved into the unconscious. This built on Nietzsche's idea that our motivations were often mysterious and opposed Descartes' view that nothing mental was hidden from the mind.

Born in what is now the Czech Republic, Freud was an Austrian. He pursued a career in neurology, the medical study of the brain. Freud began to suspect that mental illness might have its cause in the contents of a patient's mind rather than the function of the brain. His later work as a

A NEW VIEW

From the position of the psychiatrist's couch (Freud's is on the right), people were given a new view of the human condition. Before Freud, society was discussed in terms of religion, economics, and politics. After him we added psychology to the list, a paradigm shift on a scale rarely seen in history. In more recent times, however, its rigor has been questioned.

psychiatrist confirmed this. The source of problems were often stemming from a patient's disturbing desire or memory.

Making associations

Freud made a break with traditional medicine. While modern psychiatry does take Freud's work into account, it still has a physical component, using drugs to manipulate brain chemistry in an attempt to solve problems. However, Freud set out to develop a "talking cure," using the technique of free association, where patients blurted out the first thing that came into their heads in response to verbal and visual cues.

Freud believed that this would take him beyond the philosophical world of the phenomenal mind into the subconscious. His theory was that mental illness was due to thoughts locked away in the subconscious. They were too disturbing for the mind to admit, but too powerful to stay hidden.

Freud believed even healthy minds operated in the same way. We all repress our darkest desires in the subconscious "id." These interact with our rational mind, or psyche, creating the "ego." The ego is our sense of self, the pilot's seat for our minds. However, there is also a "superego," a dimly imagined mission control that steps in to override the ego on occasion, and is the main cause of mental illness.

All in the family

Freud theorized that the repressed contents of the id were the product of our earliest desires and the relationship with our parents: A boy resents the bond between his parents and wants to kill his father and marry his mother. A girl feels she has been castrated at birth and so hates her mother and her lifelong "penis envy" drives her to possess men and children. If you think this idea is shocking, Freud would say it is because your ego is protecting you from the truth. Others might look to Freud's own atypical childhood for the origins of the ideas.

Before Freud the personality was thought to have physical roots. Phrenologists thought character could be read from the shape of the head.

All Freudian psychoanalysts are taught by another Freudian and should be able to trace their knowledge back to Freud himself—a bit like Catholic bishops linking back to St. Peter (and Jesus).

FREUDIANISMS

The writings of Sigmund Freud have resulted in several interesting phrases entering informal usage: Ego, penis envy, pleasure principle, love-hate relationship. For example, the Freudian slip is where our subconscious feelings, often about sex and violence, leak out as we mis-speak about a related subject. Secondly, the term "anally retentive," or just "anal," is also used in everyday speech. Freud coined the term in relation to how people seek excessive control over their lives (and their bowels). It is used generally in a pejorative sense to mean someone needs to loosen up a bit.

Much of Freudianism revolves around the Oedipus Complex: Kill Dad, marry Mom as Oedipus did in a Greek myth, although not wholly on purpose. As a child, Freud felt unloved by his own father and was overindulged by his mother at the expense of his sisters.

61 Jungian Individuation

CARL JUNG WAS A CONTEMPORARY OF SIGMUND FREUD AND ALSO HAD AN INTEREST IN PSYCHOLOGY, the emerging science of the mind. However, the pair did not have a meeting of minds—or of unconsciousness.

Jung thought there was more to the unconscious than Freud's rather brutal view. Deeper below our personal id, he said, there lay a collective unconsciousness populated by archetypes. These were fundamental human characters such as mother, father, teacher, hero, villain, along with pivotal events, such as death, birth, and "motifs": Creation, apocalypse... Our unique selves are produced as the often contradictory unconscious entities are reconciled in the mind by a process called "individuation." Mental illness is the result of a "complex" of unconscious cues that focus on a particular problem.

Jung maintained that the collective unconsciousness was represented in mythic stories as bodies of water or even a jug. Jung was from Switzerland (which is landlocked) and he often put his archetypes beside a lake. However, this seems like as good a place as any.

62 Philosophy of Race

WILLIAM DU BOIS WAS THE FIRST AFRICAN AMERICAN TO GET A DOCTORATE FROM HARVARD UNIVERSITY. Among his achievements was to apply the all-American philosophy of pragmatism to the question of civil rights.

William du Bois was born in 1868, a few years after the Civil War, and grew up in a Massachusetts community which, for the time, was racially integrated. Only when he began his college education in Tennessee did he come up against the institutionalized racism that plagued much of the United States. And so began his lifelong struggle for his equal civil rights, which included helping to found the National Association for the Advancement of Colored People (NAACP), and a body of writings that inspired many to action, including Dr. Martin Luther King, Jr. Du Bois was a vocal opponent of scientific racism, a theory which held ground at the time that black people were a subspecies of humans, and inferior to white through their genetic makeup. (This is now utterly rebutted; all humans have genetic markers that trace their heritage to Africa.) Du Bois's philosophical legacy was based on an interpretation of pragmatism, the school of practical philosophy. In a final text written on his deathbed, he said that the "only possible death" is to lose belief in human progress. He hoped that his successes in life would survive long enough to justify his work and asked that his errors be remedied by those that follow him. In essence, he is said that it is the belief in a better life, in progress, that makes it possible to progress at all.

A belief that the future could be better was essential for those who endured the struggle to achieve U.S. civil rights.

63 Logical Positivism

BY THE 1930S, PHILOSOPHY WAS FALLING FAR BEHIND SCIENCE WHEN IT CAME TO ANSWERING QUESTIONS ABOUT THE UNIVERSE. A new, more rigorous approach to philosophy was needed.

The result was a school of thought called "logical positivism." As is perhaps fitting, it was partly inspired by the Austrian Ernst Mach, a scientist best known for Mach numbers. (Mach 1 is the speed of sound, Mach 2 is twice the speed, etc.) However, Mach's inspiration was his work on phenomenology, which said that it was only possible to gain knowledge through the senses; the mind could not do it on its own.

At a time when the likes of Albert Einstein, Ernest Rutherford, and Niels Bohr were rolling back the knowledge of space, time, and substance, philosophers working at the University of Vienna (Mach's alma mater) became disillusioned with philosophy. Much of what it offered was meaningless, they said, because it was beyond proof. It could be right, it could be wrong, but no one would ever know. To the logical positivists that made these philosophical conundrums "pseudo-problems."

So logical positivists gave up on moral questions and focused on science, checking if the theories proven by experiment also stood up to philosophical analysis. This chiefly involved ensuring the language used was unambiguous.

Rudolf Carnap was a leading figure in the logical positivist movement.

VIENNA CIRCLE

Logical positivism has a strong link with a group of philosophers who met at the University of Vienna in the 1920s. Known today as the Vienna Circle, at the time they saw themselves as members of the Ernst Mach Society, a debating group named for the recently dead Austrian physicist (below), best known for his work on the speed of sound. The gatherings included Moritz Schlick, Rudolf Carnap, and on occasion Ludwig Wittgenstein (*see* page 90). Kurt Gödel, a prodigious mathematician, was allowed to take part but not as a full member. His later incompleteness theorem (*see* page 79) would prove to be of value to both math and philosophy.

64 Schrödinger's Cat

THIS THOUGHT EXPERIMENT WAS IMAGINED BY A PHYSICIST TO QUERY A PARADOX IN THE QUANTUM THEORY. If that theory was correct, reality was no longer something we could see.

Unsurprisingly, the cat is named for that physicist, Austrian Erwin Schrödinger, who proposed it in 1935. His aim was to highlight the observer's paradox, which Schrödinger felt was a major hole in the dominant theory of quantum physics, known as the "Copenhagen interpretation."

This theory had been put together in the 1920s by various collaborators linked to a physics institute in Copenhagen. It said that the fundamental particles of nature—electrons, etc.—behaved in the same way as waves as well as particles, so were packets of mass that pinged around. The wavelike behavior was better expressed as a waveform with every characteristic of the particle expressed as in terms of probability, or the likelihood that it had a certain value. Once the particle's characteristics were measured, the waveform "collapsed" as probabilities gave way to the certainty of specific values. That idea played havoc with the concept of scientific determinism. The action of a quantum particle could result in multiple effects—and it was impossible to know which. Did that mean effects did not really have a cause? However, Schrödinger's experiment showed another problem altogether.

Put a cat in a box and close the lid. The box also contains a poison that is only released when triggered by the decay of a single radioactive atom. Radioactive decay,

IMAGINEERING

Thought experiment is a way of testing out an idea in your head. In science it can be used to frame a hypothesis and consider its merits a priori without going to the bother of actually performing it and discovering it was pointless a posteri. The term was thought up in 1812 by a scientist, Hans Christian Ørsted, the discoverer of electromagnetism. However, philosophers had been using the same technique long before that to reveal a priori knowledge of a concept. Zeno's Paradoxes and Avicenna's The Flying Man are some particularly early examples.

Both dead and alive at the same time, the cat was Erwin Schrödinger's way of exploring quantum effects in the macro-scale world of humans (and their pets).

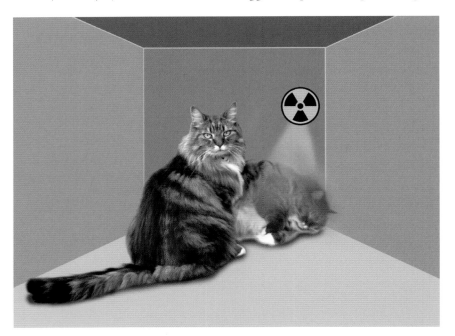

being in the realm of quantum physics, is an entirely random event. Schrödinger said that with the lid closed it is impossible to know if the cat was alive or dead. But quantum theory said that it was perfectly reasonable for it to be "dead-alive": Both states had equal probability. This is known as superposition, where substance has two or more states at once. The Copenhagen interpretation is still taught to physics students today and the evidence for it is strong. In the end the quantum world just does not conform to our customary way of thinking.

65 The Incompleteness Theorem

THIS FAMOUS BIT OF MATH IS ACTUALLY TWO THEOREMS DEVELOPED BY KURT GÖDEL. Their ramifications go beyond mere numbers.

A punched card used to input data and programming to an early computer. Gödel's theorem inspired Alan Turing and others to devise machines that could perform any function (through a list of commands) within preset limits.

There are some bold claims about Gödel's incompleteness theorem, made largely by non-mathematicians. Some say it is proof that God exists, some say it is proof he doesn't, others say it shows that the human mind will always surpass a computer. It does not really inform any of the above but once published in 1931, it had a profound impact by setting limits on knowledge.

Gödel's paper actually included two theorems about how mathematical logic is incomplete. They both refer to any formal system that can be used to express some simple arithmetic and in which some basic rules of arithmetic can be proved. That covers most of mathematics. For example, in the case of addition the rules are: $x + y = y + x$ ($2 + 1 = 3 = 1 + 2$).

The first theorem says that any *consistent* system—that is to say one that has no statements that can be proven both true and false—also contains statements that cannot be proved or disproved within the system. Secondly, no such system can be proved to be consistent within itself. For example "This statement is false" is neither true nor false. If the statement is true, then, as it says, it is false. But if it is false, then that means it must be true. The system cannot resolve itself. Gödel's theorem does the same with axioms, mathematical rules rather than statements, but it also throws light on the nature of truth and the mind for philosophers. Computers, whose development was inspired a great deal by Gödel's math, do not have the scope to work outside their limits and have no concept of having limits at all. The human mind is aware of its limits, or at least thinks it is. If it were possible to make an intelligent computer, does that mean it becomes human? Or are we really computers?

LIAR PARADOX

The Cretan philosopher Epimenides had considered self-limiting systems as far back as the 6th century BCE. He said: "I am a Cretan. All Cretans are liars." This is now called the Liar's Paradox. (Another version of it is "This sentence is false.") If it is true that all Cretans are liars, we cannot trust what Epimenides, a Cretan himself, tells us. He must be lying when he says that all Cretans are liars. And that means that some Cretans are not liars. Is Epimenides one of them? In which case he could be being honest. He really is a liar.

Kurt Gödel, with the carnation in his lapel, receives an award from Albert Einstein in 1951. Einstein had helped Gödel to escape Nazi Austria and settle in the United States.

66 The Impossibility of Truth

SCIENCE IS A SYSTEM FOR REVEALING FACTS. FOR 350 YEARS IT HAD BEEN CHANGING THE WAY we understood our place in the Universe. Then in 1934 Karl Popper pointed out that science had not actually proven anything at all!

You can be certain that what goes up must come down, but does this prove it?

Science is a way of investigating natural phenomena, what David Hume called the "regularities of nature." It is entirely empirical, based only on what can be experienced through the senses, and a system of units has been devised to ensure that all records of all scientists' experiences conform to the same standards and are thus comparable. So far so good, and by the 1930s the scientific method was thought to be well understood: First a scientist would think of a question about a phenomenon. Next they would carry out background research before proposing a hypothesis, or explanation. That hypothesis was then tested using an experiment, the results of which show whether the hypothesis is true or false. If the former, the scientist announces his or her discovery to the world: A new truth has been found.

Reasonable falsehoods

Karl Popper was interested in the hypothesis and experiment, especially the latter. He wanted to know the reasoning used to show how a result proved a hypothesis true or false. If an experiment relied on inductive reasoning, it was doomed to fail. For example, to test the statement: "Stones always sink in water," an experiment might be to drop a stone into some water. Is it reasonable to assume it will sink? Yes? But what about the next stone? It is probable

EXPECT THE UNEXPECTED

Popper's critique of scientific truth shows that just because something has never happened—or been observed to happen—does not mean it is untrue. This is the flaw in inductive reasoning. In 16th-century Europe, induction would have "proven" that all swans were white. A century later, and a quick voyage to the newly found Australia would have shown swans could be black too. Today "black swan" is used as the term of something unlikely but entirely possible.

that you have never seen a stone not sink in water, but Popper said that does not mean the statement is true. Inductive reasoning takes a particular case—your experience of sinking stones—and generalizes it. (Pumice stones are often light enough to float.) Popper said that a hypothesis can only

AND THE WORLD TURNS

According to Popper's doctrine of falsifiability, we had no proof that Earth spun on its axis until 1851. Until then the best evidence we had—the motion of the rising Sun—relied on inductive reasoning. In 1851, Frenchman Léon Foucault set up a huge pendulum in Paris and set it swinging over some compass points on the floor. It was known that pendulums always swing in the same plane, but this one appeared to rotate slowly, sweeping over the compass points throughout the day. However, it was not the pendulum that moved, but the Earth spinning beneath it.

be validated if it is proven using deductive reasoning. This takes a general point—mammals have hair—and uses it to inform a particular case. So if Grandpa is hairy you can deduce beyond all doubt that he is a mammal. However, Popper realized we can never get away from induction. We can never say that the hypothesis "All grandpas are mammals" is scientifically true. A scientist can only agree that the hypothesis has yet to be proven false—and perhaps one day it will be. However, until that day, science can treat the hypothesis as valid in the continued study of grandpas.

67 Language, Truth and Logic

AS A YOUNG MAN IN THE 1930S, THE ENGLISH PHILOSOPHER AJ AYER WAS INVITED TO JOIN THE VIENNA CIRCLE. FROM WHAT HE LEARNED THERE, he decided that much of philosophy was meaningless gibberish.

A.J. Ayer was a maverick. In 1987, aged 77, he was able to face down an angry Mike Tyson at a party in New York. Ayer pointed out that they were both preeminent, one the heavyweight champion of the world, the other the former Wykeham Professorship of Logic.

A large part of philosophy is the study of metaphysics. That word refers by definition to things that are beyond our senses—Hegel's Spirit, Kant's noumenal world, Jung's archetypes. Ayer said it was all nonsense. As for the rest of philosophy he applied the Verification Principle. This asked 1) Is it true by definition? If not 2) Is it empirically verifiable? If you got a second no, then the statement was meaningless and should be ignored. This test is an updated version of Hume's Fork. If a statement fails it need not be useless, though. Its failure can indicate a change that will give it some meaning: "All boats have sails" is unverifiable, but "Some boats have sails" is. Ayer also gave a caveat to ethical philosophy. To say stealing is wrong, giving to charity is right, was to simply offer an opinion, not state a truth. Or as he put it himself, it is akin to saying, "Stealing, boo! Charity, hooray!"

68 Marcuse: Truth is False

BY THE MIDDLE OF THE 20TH CENTURY, PHILOSOPHY WAS TRICKLING DOWN TO THE MAINSTREAM. The man and woman on the street were in touch with ideas about rationality, reason, and logic. The German-American philosopher Herbert Marcuse could not help but be suspicious.

In 1941, Marcuse published *Reason and Revolution* in which he challenged an idea most associated with Georg Hegel: Human progress is based on reason, and therefore our societies are rational. Marcuse did not think so. Instead, he suggested that beneath the varnish of rationality which people apply to the social and political zeitgeist are emotion and fantasy—deep down we are irrational beings.

Marcuse's critique was made in a general attack on the idea of basing society on capitalism, which he said offered a "terrifying harmony of freedom and oppression, productivity and destruction, growth, and regression." He said that people find their "soul" through consumption of products and are represented by what they buy. In doing so, we assume that the social, economic, political, and justice systems that underwrite this way of living is based on reason—and we only have Hegel's word for that. Marcuse was no philosophical skeptic. However, he saw philosophy's aim as developing a theory of society, rather than creating society itself.

69 Absurd Camus

ALBERT CAMUS, A FRENCH WRITER AND REBEL, IS OFTEN DESCRIBED AS AN EXISTENTIALIST. But Camus would have said this was absurd, and so was everything else.

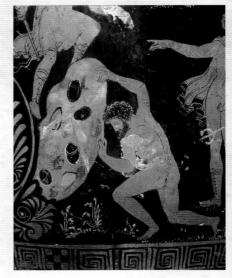

Albert Camus espoused much of his philosophy in the form of plays and novels, many of which have become cult classics, such as *L'Étranger* (*The Stranger*) and the *Myth of Sisyphus*. This second work encapsulated his philosophy, which he described as the "paradox of the absurd." It stemmed from the observation that even when a person reasons that their life—ending in inescapable death—is ultimately futile, they still maintain that it has value (to them at least). Sisyphus was condemned by the gods to push a rock up a hill every day, only to see it roll back down to the bottom, and so he started again. In Camus's retelling, Sisyphus finds happiness in this single act of existence. Camus argued that one must embrace the meaninglessness of our own lives—which are hopefully more varied than that of Sisyphus—and not seek to evade their inherent absurdity with clever, logic-based systems to "create a meaning."

King Sisyphus, according to Greek myth, was something of a despotic psychokiller—until, that is, Zeus sent him to the underworld to move the rocks around for eternity.

70 Jean-Paul Sartre

AT ITS HEART, PHILOSOPHY IS IN SEARCH OF A DESCRIPTION OF HUMAN NATURE, OF WHAT IT MEANS TO BE HUMAN. Jean-Paul Sartre, one of the most iconic philosophers of the 20th century, suggested that if human nature were to be described fully we would be losing part of our humanity in the process.

Sartre was an existentialist, and it is with his work that we get the fullest understanding of that term. The search for the essence of what it is to be a human is predicated on the idea that some feature applies equally to all of us and has remained unchanged though history. However, Sartre believed that a human's ability to choose our own nature was central to this essence—and we don't all automatically choose the same things.

A popular uprising inspired by Sartre and others in 1968 in France led to the fall of the government and ushered in a more liberal political climate that is still evident today.

Existence versus essence

Now comes the existentialist bit: The essence of an object comes before its existence. Sartre uses a knife as an example. A knife is crafted to perform a certain purpose. Whatever material you use, it always requires a certain length and sharpness. Religion proposes that humans are crafted along the same lines, only by the gods. As a staunch atheist, Sartre did not stand for this proposition, saying that religion permeated deeply into secular thinking. Instead, he said that unlike objects, the existence of a human precedes the essence. We are not made for a purpose, but are free to choose one for ourselves. While our choices were our own, Sartre was aware that every individual choice had an impact on humanity at large. In his later career as a political and social firebrand, the responsibility of freedom was central to Sartre's message.

Jean-Paul Sartre's philosophy was a major influence on the protest movements of the 1960s.

71 The Second Sex

FROM THE OUTSET, PHILOSOPHY HAS BEEN PRACTICED BY MEN AND SO IS ABOUT MEN. SO SAID SIMONE DE BEAUVOIR, THE FRENCH PHILOSOPHER AND AUTHOR, who became the touchstone for the feminist movement of the late 20th century.

Simone de Beauvoir was the author of *The Second Sex*, published in 1949, which is regarded as the seminal feminist work. And straight away we have an example of its major theme: Society as a whole, from its customs to language, let alone philosophy, is imbued with maleness. The word *seminal*, used here to describe how modern feminism grew from de Beauvoir's book, is derived from the Latin for "seed" and also refers to semen, the major contribution of a male in the creation of new life. We've described the foundations of feminism with a male term.

Aristotle was clear in his views—only men were fully human—and while later philosophers would not have agreed with him, man remained "the measure of all things." In other words, the standard condition was the male one, against which all new philosophies and new outlooks were sized up.

DEFINED WOMAN

In a male-dominated society, de Beauvoir described how women were defined by men, largely in how they differ from the male standard. In ancient Greece, women were aligned with the mystery of nature—beyond reason, unpredictable, and irresistibly alluring. Modern female identity has retained much of this confusing mix with women expected (by men) to be both sexy, chaste, caring, and exciting all at the same time.

In de Beauvoir's time, the female role model was always found at home, caring for the family and being cared for by men.

I and the Other

De Beauvoir pointed out that philosophers often talk about the "self," but here again that concept is described from the male point of view. A male philosopher cannot talk about what he understands as "I" in any other way. De Beauvoir stated that a female self is equivalent but different, saying that where the male self is "I," the female is "Other."

At the heart of this concept is a clarification of previous calls for sexual equality made by the likes of Mary Wollstonecraft and John Stuart Mill: The equality of women is judged according to how they are like men. It is not enough to say that women should be treated equally as men because that does not take into account that the two sexes are different, and have different ideas of self.

Simone de Beauvoir said notions of femininity were constructed by men, as typified by this Christian Dior design from 1949, the year of publication of The Second Sex.

Female experience

As a philosopher, de Beauvoir took a phenomenological approach, that is to say, she sought to understand reality from the experiences perceived by the mind—or the self. She said everyone learned to understand the world in their own way, but de Beauvoir argued that the world as perceived by a man is fundamentally different to how it was experienced by a woman. The "self" of a man was formed within the body that formed its interface with the rest of the Universe. A woman interacts with the Universe with a different body, and the "other" that is created within is also different.

Simone de Beauvoir spent her life with Jean-Paul Sartre, although they were never formally married. Commenting on the arrangement, de Beauvoir said, "Marriage was impossible. I had no dowry."

While still at college, Simone de Beauvoir met Jean-Paul Sartre, who would become her partner and was also the leading male French philosopher of his generation. Like Sartre, de Beauvoir was an existentialist and subscribed to his philosophy that human nature was not a fixed idea but something that every person created for themselves. Therefore, by fusing two ideas together, de Beauvoir argued that it was up to every woman to figure out how to live their life, to carve out a role for themselves. It was not effective for women to merely aim to behave like men, and the goal was all the harder because it meant disregarding the customary notions of womanhood that had been developed over generations by male-dominated society.

> *"One is not born but becomes a woman."*
>
> DE BEAUVOIR

Female or feminine

De Beauvoir drew a distinction between having a female anatomy and behaving in a feminine manner. The former was the product of biology, the latter was constructed by society and was an impossible set of ideals that kept women as passive individuals, who could hope for, at best, the approval of men. At the start of *The Second Sex*, she says, "We are exhorted to be women, remain women, become women. It would appear, then, that every female human being is not necessarily a woman."

So what is the authentic "other nature" of female human beings? And is the corollary of de Beauvoir's philosophy that men should also reconsider their sense of self?

72 Ryle's Behavior

BE CAREFUL WHAT YOU SAY, PEOPLE MIGHT GET THE WRONG IDEA ABOUT YOU.
English philosopher Gilbert Ryle was a behaviorist who believed that we understand each other through observing our actions, not our mental activity, and in order to do that he needed to correct a very old mistake.

Gilbert Ryle liked to compare ideas with information displayed on maps. One example of a category mistake is to look for a city among its buildings. The city and its buildings are not in the same category and must be analyzed differently.

In 1949, Ryle said that since the days of Descartes, philosophies of the mind had been laboring under a misapprehension. Descartes was a dualist, which meant he believed that the mind and the body were separate, and this informed much of the way philosophers had viewed the mind ever since. Ryle called this view "the ghost in the machine." He coined the term "category mistake" to explain why.

Body before mind
He said the mind and body cannot be discussed using the same terms. The dualist "ghost" concept describes the mind as a distinct thing that controls the body, making it move and talk, etc. That puts the mind and the body in the same category of things. However, Ryle argued that to say that "Meredith has a questioning mind" did not mean we can observe her mind and hear it produce a string of questions. Instead, our characterization of Meredith is the result of experiencing her inquisitive behavior. In reality, what we talk about as "the mind" is composed of the activities of the body. It is wrong to think that thinking itself, or wishing, hoping, and believing are activities in a nonmaterial form. They are processes within the material brain. Therefore, you cannot say the mind and body are two distinct things. Any system of philosophy that treats them as such is making a category mistake, which creates a "ghost in the machine" that can never be studied and understood. In Ryle's words: "The Ghost in the Machine maintains that there exist both bodies and minds; that there occur physical processes and mental processes; that there are mechanical causes of corporeal movements and mental causes of corporeal movements. I shall argue that these and other analogous conjunctions are absurd."

See what you mean
Ryle set out his ideas in the book, *Concept of Mind,* in 1949. This category mistake had far-reaching consequences, Ryle argued. It means that when we talk about a person's mental state, we tend to understand it as being something held inside a distinct entity, somewhere inside of the body, but separate from it. In turn, that suggests the body has two masters: the thoughts of the mind and the physical mechanics that operate it. Ryle's central point was that this is an unnecessary dichotomy that has arisen from the language used to describe consciousness. To Ryle, mind and body were one and the same thing.

> *"Minds are not merely ghosts harnessed to machines, they are themselves just spectral machines."*
> RYLE

73 Russell on Work

BERTRAND RUSSELL BEGAN HIS CAREER AS A MATHEMATICIAN, SEEKING TO REDUCE HIS SUBJECTS TO FIRST PRINCIPLES. He then turned those same analytical skills to the philosophy of work.

Bertrand Russell was not lazy but had an unusual attitude to work: "Moving matter about is not one of the goals of human life," he said. However, being a British aristocrat—the 3rd Earl Russell—gave him plenty of time to think about it.

Russell (and his coauthor Alfred North Whitehead) famously took more than 700 pages of their book, *Principia Mathematica,* to prove that 1+1=2. Russell's later analysis of work was a lot shorter but no less rigorous. He said there were two kinds of work. The first was "altering the position of matter on or near to the Earth's surface relative to other matter." The second kind of work was "telling other people to alter the position of matter relative to other such matter." In so doing, Russell defines two types of worker, the laborer and the supervisor (with some supervisors supervising other supervisors). The working class are poorly paid for hard work while the supervisory middle class are better paid for having less-physical duties. There is a third "upper" class, who do no work at all, but depend on the labors of the other two groups to fund their life of leisure. Since the dawn of history, the upper class, who collect the surplus wealth produced by work, had preached the virtues of hard work. Russell's simple proposal was to reevaluate the value of working. His conclusion was that a route out of poverty through "honest toil" only served to promote oppression. Instead, we should rebalance our lives, reduce work to a minimum, and take leisure—including education—just as seriously.

HISTORIC WESTERN PHILOSOPHER

In the late 1940s, Bertrand Russell published *History of Western Philosophy,* a compendium of philosophy ranging from the dawn of Greek civilization to James Dewey. It remains one of the best-selling philosophy books to this day. Russell completed the book in his early 70s, but his career was far from over. If anything his politics became more radical with age. At the age of 89, he was sentenced to a week in prison for civil disobedience during an antinuclear protest. In his 90s, he settled down and wrote his autobiography— it ran to three volumes.

Bertrand Russell first expounded his theories on work during the Great Depression, when one in three people in Europe and America were destitute. The depression was a product of an unevaluated work ethic, was Russell's analysis.

74 Anthropic Principle

PHILOSOPHY ATTEMPTS TO DESCRIBE DIFFERENT WAYS IN WHICH THE HUMAN EXPERIENCE DEFINES THE UNIVERSE. IN THE EARLY 1950S, cosmologists, scientists who study the formation of the Universe, were putting together the fundamental laws that make our Universe exist. The next question was this: Are we only conscious of the Universe because of its basic laws?

By the 1930s, it had become obvious that the Solar System was nowhere near the center of the Milky Way, and the principle of mediocrity took hold. This states that our Sun, Solar System, and its life-bearing planet are nothing unusual. All life needs are the laws of physics and chemistry plus the right conditions for a primordial soup to cook up some biochemical entities that grow and reproduce. What is needed is often called a Goldilocks orbit—a place in space that is not too hot, not too cold, but just right. However, there is more to it than that.

The laws of the Universe are just right for life. If they were adjusted even slightly, stable stars, planets, and complex chemical-based life-forms would become impossible. For example, the electromagnetic force which holds atoms together is 10^{39} times stronger than gravity. Therefore, the two forces work together to make clouds of gases compress and ignite into stars, and those stars then burn their fuels at a rate slow enough for stable planetary systems to form around them. The planets then need to survive long enough (billions of years) for life to evolve into an intelligent civilization capable of understanding—or attempting to understand—its place in the Universe.

COPERNICAN PRINCIPLE

By definition we live in an anthropic Universe—we would not be here otherwise. However, the Austrian-British astronomer Hermann Bondi proposed another way of looking at it: The Copernican Principle states that we are not the center of the Solar System (as revealed below by Nicholas Copernicus in the 16th century) and our Sun is not even close to the center of the galaxy. As such, Earth and humanity are an inconsequential part of an immense, expanding Universe.

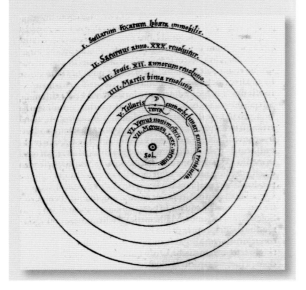

A planned system

So the next question is whether the Universe we observe is the way it is, because it has to be like that for us to exist and to observe it? To some that suggests that the Universe must have been tuned to be "anthropic," meaning suitable for humanity, and that is evidence of a creator, who brought the Universe into being. Another way of looking at this Anthropic Principle is that there are (and have been) many universes, some of which have laws of physics that are incompatible with life. Our Universe is one of the minority, or perhaps the only one, that has intelligent life and, therefore, has observers to take notice of it. Whether accident or design, does the principle tell us anything?

> *"Like Baby Bear's porridge in the story of Goldilocks, the Universe seems to be just right for life."*
>
> PAUL DAVIES, PHYSICIST

75 The Turing Test

ALAN TURING WAS AN ENGLISH MATHEMATICIAN THOUGHT BY MANY TO BE THE FATHER OF COMPUTERS. His contribution was a hypothetical device that could follow instructions. Could such a device be made to think like a human being?

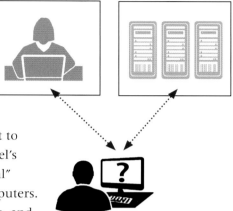

The Turing Machine is the name used to describe the device that Alan Turing proposed in the late 1930s. It was meant as a thought experiment to investigate the limits of mathematical systems, as described by Kurt Gödel's Incompleteness Theorems. However, by the 1950s, the "virtual" machine had become real as the basis of early electronic computers. It worked by reading instructions from an infinitely long tape, and acting on them in accordance with a preordained set of rules, or algorithm. As the electronic age began, people began to wonder if that was how we also think, and whether an algorithm could be written to emulate the workings of the human mind. If so, would the computer be really thinking?

The Turing Test is generally carried out by typing questions onto a screen. The interrogator is given five minutes to figure out who or what they are talking to.

In response, Turing suggested it did not matter how the intelligence was arrived at, merely how clever it was. He proposed a test: A human interrogates two entities unseen in other rooms. One is another human, the other is a computer. If the interrogator is unable to tell which one is the human, then the computer is deemed to possess artificial intelligence (AI).

In recent years, there have been many competitions based on this Turing Test, where entrants from around the world enter their AI programs. While some have proven better than others—for example, by reflecting questions they cannot answer back at the interviewer—so far, no computer has passed the test.

The Chinese Room

In 1980, American philosopher John Searle pointed out a flaw in the Turing Test. He said that a computer capable of passing the test was akin to a non-Chinese person being given Chinese characters to create written answers to questions also written in Chinese. They had all the instructions needed to correlate the symbols and produce an answer, so could pass the test. So a computer could follow similar rules to beat the test but would be unaware of the process and would not really be thinking.

THE TURK

In 1770, Wolfgang von Kempelen, a Hungarian inventor, unveiled The Turk, a mechanical chess player. He toured the royal courts of Europe with it, where his mechanical robot regularly beat humans at chess. Many believed Kempelen had built an intelligent machine. The figure, styled in Turkish garb, moved pieces with its mechanical arm. Before each game, Kempelen showed off the complex mechanisms inside the chest—much of which was empty space. Of course, it was all a trick. The base contained a small but very skilled chess master, who slid into a hiding place during inspections of the interior.

76 Wittgenstein: Saying the Unsayable

LUDWIG WITTGENSTEIN DID NOT BELIEVE IN LEARNING PHILOSOPHY FROM BOOKS. HOWEVER, SINCE WE ARE HERE, you may as well ignore him and find out a bit more about this Austrian genius, the greatest philosopher of his generation.

Wittgenstein's primary contribution to philosophy was a work that took form while he was serving in the Austrian army on the Russian and Italian fronts of the World War I. (He became a prisoner a week before the Great War ended, and remained in an Italian camp for nine months before his release was processed.) The resulting book was *Tractatus Logico-Philosophicus* (Latin for *Logical-Philosophical Treatise*), finally published in 1921.

It was only short—just around 70 pages—and it read like the cross between a book of poetry and a computer program. In it Wittgenstein set out seven propositions, and he then analyzed each one in a rather gnomic way. The broad thrust of the book was that earlier philosophy was hindered by a misunderstanding of language. A few philosophers, notably Bertrand Russell and the Vienna Circle, were inspired by the logical rigor of this, Wittgenstein's first work. However, it was a later book, *Philosophical Investigations*, published in 1953, a couple of years after the philosopher's death, which encapsulated his final approach, and clarified earlier work.

Ludwig Wittgenstein remains one of the most influential, but also mysterious of philosophers.

Bewitchment of language

Wittgenstein likened the philosopher to a fly in a bottle, slamming itself into the glass in an attempt to get outside to explore the world. The barrier is the way people use

WRITING WORDS

The confusion, or misconception, about the nature of language may be based in the written word. Writing has been developed independently several times over the last 8,000 years, and each time it results in symbols being used to represent words. This is achieved either by having symbols for objects or ideas, or using symbols for the sounds of spoken words. The effect is the same—each word becomes a label for a specific meaning.

Cuneiform, the writing system developed by Mesopotamian cultures, used wedge marks in wet clay.

language. Surely words are mere labels for things? That is the essence, or underlying common basis, of all languages. However, Wittgenstein refused to accept this concept. Instead, he argued that one word could be used in several ways, each way sharing a few of a set of common features. He described this as a family of meanings, in the same way members of families resemble each other in different ways, although no two look entirely the same.

Public and private

Language has to be public, shared and affirmed by people as a whole. Private words, used by one person only, are meaningless because there is no way of confirming what was meant. Wittgenstein's typically strange example was a beetle in a box. If we all kept a beetle inside a box, but never showed it to anyone else, would it be valid to call it a beetle? If no one ever checked it was indeed a beetle, and not a worm or rock or whatever, the word *beetle* was not a valid term for whatever we had hidden away.

Similarly, Wittgenstein applied the same logic to how we communicate our sensations, such as pain. He described how an entirely private event, such as experiencing a certain itch or tingle, could be given the label S by a philosopher. Every time that person feels the same sensation, they describe it as S. However, without a public confirmation that the second sensation is the same as the first—and not slightly different in some way—the term S is just an imprecise meaningless noise, like "ouch" or indeed "I've got an itch."

So with that said, we can understand more about Wittgenstein's initial statement from *Tractatus*: "The world is all that is the case." On the face of it an obvious statement, but what Wittgenstein meant was that the world is composed only of propositions that can be communicated by unambiguous "perfect" language: "Wittgenstein is dead" is a full proposition that can be considered either true or false, and is thus part of the world. "Wittgenstein" alone is not a valid proposition and is thus not something that can be considered. In so doing, Wittgenstein established the limits of language, which meant that it was not possible to discuss questions beloved of philosophy. Unless, that is, the mind was not private at all, and there is some public consciousness linking us all.

Wittgenstein used the duck-rabbit illusion to investigate the way we see things. We can report what we see— seeing that it is a duck, for example, or you could note that you can see it as both a duck and a rabbit. Wittgenstein was interested in the internal process whereby the second possible label arose from the first.

"Like everything metaphysical, the harmony between thought and reality is to be found in the grammar of the language."

WITTGENSTEIN

77 Riddle of Induction

IN 1955, AN AMERICAN PHILOSOPHER RETURNED TO THE PROBLEM OF INDUCTION THAT DAVID HUME HAD TACKLED 200 YEARS BEFORE. Nelson Goodman took the idea to its extreme, creating the "new riddle of induction" in which he was able to show that green was also blue, eventually.

The ruby on the left is red, while the emerald is green. That matches all the other rubies and emeralds you've ever seen—up till now. However, they are both gred and reen, and perhaps even blreen as well!

In his classical problem of induction, Hume exposed the folly of assuming that future events could be predicted from past observations. However, doing so had its uses, and society bases its customs on these "regularities" of nature—not least night following day, and so forth. The assumption was that regular events were the product of some kind of universal law. However, Goodman wanted to know how credible a custom was. How can you tell if a regularity is based on a law of nature or is just the product of a random coincidence? Following Hume's thinking, both cases could be used to establish a custom. So, a snowflake being cold would lead to an understanding that all snowflakes are cold, but also rolling a die a few times and getting a six does not mean that it is true to say that dice always land on sixes.

Hypothesis versus evidence

Carl Hempel, a contemporary of Goodman, suggested that you could tell law-based truth from coincidence by checking if it could be used as a hypothesis: Snow is made of frozen water and therefore it is cold. If this is not possible, then the observation is just evidence of an event: A die lands on six, one of the possible sides it can lie on. (Hempel was also responsible for the Raven paradox: Every time you see an object that is not black nor a raven, then the chance that ravens are black goes up.) However, Goodman was not convinced by the division between hypothesis and evidence, and his counterargument became famous.

Emeralds are grue

Goodman proposed the following hypothesis: Something is grue when it appears green when checked before a fixed future moment (time t), and appears blue after that moment. Therefore, all emeralds are grue. The rule of induction tells us that emeralds have always been green, and therefore they will also be green after time t. However, our hypothesis says that emeralds will appear blue at this time. Observing emeralds are green prior to t only confirms the hypothesis. A green emerald in your hand lends equal evidential weight to the statements "All emeralds are green" and "All emeralds are grue." The idea that emeralds are grue is obviously nonsense, yet the logic behind it is indistinguishable from logic that emeralds will always be green.

"Truth cannot be defined or tested by agreement with 'the world.'"

GOODMAN

78 Theoretical Linguistics

"Humans have properties which are intrinsic to them, just as every other organism does."

CHOMSKY

LANGUAGE IS CENTRAL TO THE WORK OF A PHILOSOPHER. IN THE MID-1950S, NOAM CHOMSKY launched into the debate on how language works, resurrecting ideas of innate knowledge and an essence of language.

In 1955, Noam Chomsky, then a twentysomething linguist, published the first volume of *Syntactic Structures*. It revolutionized the way people have since approached the study of language—although the ideas in it still have many opponents. Chomsky's approach was to treat language as a biological phenomenon. He suggested that there is a common structure to human language that is present at birth, encoded and passed on by the genes. The result is a universal grammar, a system of organization that can be found within every language, which every human already "knows" at birth.

Chomsky was inspired by the work of Panini, an ancient Indian linguist, who worked in Sanskrit, a language from which many European and Asian languages have evolved. Therefore, Chomsky's work is open to criticism in being overly focused on the Indo–European languages, and having a tendency to frame all other languages in the same way, despite them having immense differences.

Pre-acquired understanding

This is not to say that we all know how to speak from birth, and are discovering what we already knew (as Plato might have thought). Instead, Chomsky proposed (his work on the subject continued over the following 20 years) that humans have a language acquisition device (LAD), a hypothetical mechanism in the brain, that allows us to learn to understand and use language by listening to the people around us. In the first few weeks and months of life, a puppy and a human baby have similar cognitive abilities (the human begins to outstrip the dog around the age of four), but only the human will go on to develop language, all due to the LAD, Chomksy said. How else could a child develop comprehensible language skills that exceed its experience? Despite the "poverty of stimulus" we can understand a lot more than what we've already heard before.

To be or not to be? A linguist would check the grammar first.

	affirmative	negative	question
I	I am	I am not	Am I?
he/she/it	He is	He is not	Is he?
you/we/they	You are	You are not	Are you?

79 Heidegger's Self-Analysis

THE GERMAN MARTIN HEIDEGGER WAS INTERESTED IN THE AGE-OLD QUESTION: WHAT IS IT TO BE A HUMAN BEING? His answer was that humans are the only beings who are interested in that question.

DEATH BECOMES US

Central to Martin Heidegger's philosophy is our realization of death looming ever closer. He said that any attempt to understand what it is to be human will come to an end with death—and this is a large part of what makes us human.

Active between the late 1920s to the late 1950s, Heidegger was no different to other philosophers in wanting to distill the essence of what it meant to be human. However, his approach to doing so was different, and earned him a place as one of the 20th century's leading thinkers. Heidegger was a phenomenologist, meaning he viewed reality in terms of the phenomena, or experiences, perceived by the human mind. And he chose to address the question of human nature from that viewpoint as well.

Because he believed that it was only possible to understand what existed (and what didn't) by the phenomena of our experiences, he came to realize that to analyze what it was to be human, to be ourselves, was also the way to analyze the existence of everything else. It struck him that the thing that made human beings different to other life-forms was that humans wonder about their own existence. We are all born into the middle of history already in train and which directs the course of our lives. We attempt to comprehend our lives through occupations and education, and in turn we try to guide our lives towards a particular future state, or goal, which gives meaning to our existence. However, we eventually become aware that our being will end at some point, irrespective of the goals we set. To ignore this fact is to live, as termed by Heidegger, inauthentically. An authentic life must accept the limits of our being.

Education is a means to an end according to Heidegger's analysis, giving us the opportunity to live authentically.

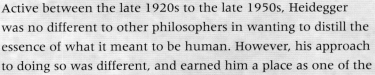

80 Many Worlds Theory

MANY PHILOSOPHERS HAVE COMMENTED ON THE IDEA OF CAUSALITY, WHICH PONDERS HOW EVERY EFFECT HAS A CAUSE. In 1957, a physicist entered the fray by suggesting that one cause could have many effects.

The man in question was Hugh Everett, an American quantum physicist. He was dissatisfied with the main branch of quantum mechanics which pulls a veil over cause and effect. Put simply, it states that the material in the Universe is made up of a family of subatomic particles. Every particle is expressed as a jumbled wave of probabilities (*see* box). When an effect occurs—an observable and measurable event—this waveform is said to have "collapsed" into a set of precise characteristics. The uncertainty of this mechanism means that there is no way of making a direct connection between a cause and its effect. The element of chance means that one cause could have many effects, so the consensus is that there is no way of predicting which effect will arise from which cause.

Everett put forward the "many worlds theory." This proposes that the waveform does not collapse, and so all the possible outcomes it contains each produce an effect. That means any effect we observe being caused is just one of many effects that have the same cause but are occurring in other universes. The number of these parallel universes is always on the increase as the timeline splits into alternative branches where these alternative events are taking place. Everett was certainly a maverick. He died young due to overeating and alcoholism. However, he would contend that a version of him is still alive—and always will be—in at least one alternative universe.

A philosophical consequence of quantum physics is that our objective reality is just one infinitesimal part of nature at large, which is made up of a growing number of alternative versions of our reality,

WAVEFORMS AND PARTICLES

The word *particle* is used more for convenience than anything else, because at the subatomic level they do not behave like the dots of solid matter that the word suggests. Instead, their characteristics, such as spin and location, are uncertain and expressed as a waveform of probabilities. In other words, the characteristics are not fixed, just more likely to be one value than another. The act of measuring the characteristics will collapse the waveform into specific values. Albert Einstein was not impressed with this idea, saying: "God does not play dice."

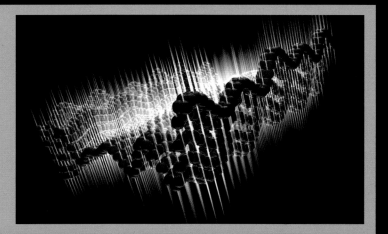

81 Berlin and Freedom

FREEDOM IS A THEME THAT RUNS THROUGH MODERN LIFE. WE ALL WANT TO BE FREE, WE SAY, BUT WHAT DOES THAT MEAN? In the late 1950s, Isaiah Berlin found a contradiction at the heart of this most human desire. Does freedom always lead to a good life?

In some senses freedom is easy to define. But then again it is very difficult to pin down what it is. In 1958, Isaiah Berlin entered the debate by splitting the concept in two. Berlin, who grew up in Russia during its revolutionary period, had witnessed the oppression of the Tsarist regime replaced with the oppression of the communists—all in the name of freedom—and so the subject was an enduring theme in his work.

Freedom from incarceration is one of our most primitive urges, but there are other ways to be free.

Positive and negative

Berlin termed the two types of freedom as positive and negative. Negative freedom is the one that we think of first. Berlin called it our "fundamental sense" of what freedom is. Negative freedom is to be free of an external object, such as the walls of prison or the unwanted attention of another person. In other words, it is freedom from something. However, simply unlocking a door is not the only thing that makes us free. There is positive freedom as well.

Berlin's positive freedom is more nuanced. It is freedom to do something, freedom to choose how we live our lives, the ability to determine what we are. Berlin also believed that positive freedom could be ascribed to groups of people, even entire countries.

Opposite forces

But being free gets complicated. Using the positive freedom to opt to learn a skill, such as to play tennis, means you must spend many hours practicing—and so lose negative freedom. Similarly, the positive choice to vote for a leader results in a restriction of negative freedom as we must do as he or she says. In the end, says Berlin, all choices result in conflicts and there are no absolute rules on the best way to live.

ARE YOU A HEDGEHOG OR A FOX?

Isaiah Berlin came to prominence through his 1953 essay, *The Hedgehog and the Fox*. Within it Berlin discussed how thinkers fall into two groups: Hedgehogs are those who have one big idea and rely on it to explain everything. The foxes juggle many different ideas, even contradictory ones, to achieve the same goal.

82 Paradigm Shifts

THE PHRASE "PARADIGM SHIFT" IS NOW MUCH MALIGNED AS A BLAND MANAGEMENT SPEAK, BUT WHEN IT WAS INTRODUCED BY the American philosopher Thomas Kuhn, it had an important point to make about how we push back the boundaries of our knowledge.

"Normal science does not aim at novelties of fact or theory and, when successful, finds none."

KUHN

Kuhn was a professional scientist who saw a fundamental pattern in the course of the history of science. This idea formed the basis of his 1962 book, *The Structure of Scientific Revolutions.* Kuhn was interested in the impact of the greatest scientific discoveries which occur from time to time over recent centuries, such as Nicolaus Copernicus proving Earth orbits the Sun or Albert Einstein linking matter and energy in his theory of relativity. These breakthroughs appear to overturn the established thinking of the scientific community, and redirect research on a new course. Kuhn was interested in what this process told us about the nature of knowledge.

Most of the time, according to Kuhn, the boundaries of knowledge are unfurled using "normal science," through a succession of observations, theories, and experiments. These all comply with an agreed framework, or set of rules, about the nature of the subjects being studied, which Kuhn called the paradigm. History shows that every paradigm collects an increasing number of mysterious results which do not comply with it. Eventually, these anomalies build up to such an extent that there is what Kuhn terms a scientific "crisis." From the crisis emerges a new discovery which changes the paradigm, and "normal" science resumes within this new framework.

One of Kuhn's observations is that during the normal period, scientists search for truths that conform with the paradigm. Only during crises will they begin to entertain novel ideas that might involve shifting the paradigm. This opens up questions of relativism: Scientific truth is only true in relation to the current paradigm. And if that stops working, then science will come up with a new one. To many commentators that would suggest that scientific knowledge is driven along in nonrational steps. How can we be certain that a new paradigm is a more accurate representation of reality?

During a scientific crisis, people are forced to look outside of their current theoretical framework—the foundation upon which scientific knowledge had been based to that point.

83 Habermas on Society

JURGEN HABERMAS WAS A CHILD DURING THE NAZI REGIME THAT RULED HIS NATIVE GERMANY IN THE 1930S AND 1940S. As an adult his philosophy was heavily influenced by that time, specifically its lack of public criticism. Habermas went on to analyze how societies monitor themselves.

What defines modern society? Is it our ability to cure disease, communicate with each other, or develop and manufacture ever more useful technologies? Habermas proposed that it was more than that. Hand in hand with its technological developments, a modern society is also one that is able to examine and criticize itself. Habermas had been witness to the Nazi regime, a society that was at the cutting edge of the technological abilities of its day but one that had no ability to challenge developments.

In 1962, Habermas expanded on this theme by saying that just as a modern society required reason to develop technologically, it required a "communicative" reason to progress socially. This took the form of ordinary people being able to question the ruling class, if not directly, then among themselves in what Habermas called the "third space." A free press is a major bastion of the third space, as a means of holding rulers to account. But in his later years, Habermas questioned whether traditional outlets for journalism are still fulfilling this role or have become arms of the entertainment industry.

THE THIRD SPACE

Habermas's third space is a public sphere between the private family space and the infrastructure of government. He traces its emergence back to the 18th-century coffeehouses of Europe, where people gathered to discuss matters of the day (below). He suggests that these establishments were crucial for the transition of European societies from "representational" cultures (where the rulers just displayed their power) to today's communicative ones.

84 Foucault's Invented Humanity

BY THE 1960S, IT WAS BECOMING WELL ESTABLISHED THAT THE MODERN HUMAN SPECIES was a relative newcomer to life on Earth. The French philosopher Michel Foucault wondered how that changed the way we could understand our distant ancestors.

> *"Man is neither the oldest nor the most constant problem that has been posed for human knowledge."*
>
> FOUCAULT

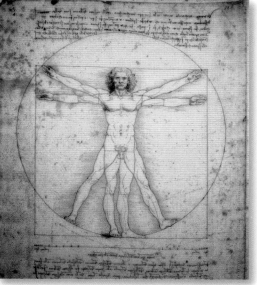

In 1966, Foucault's book, *The Order of Things*, returned to the debate over the genesis of human nature and how that impacts on our ideas of what it is to be a human being. Like many philosophers before him, Foucault recognized that the way a human relates to his or her surroundings, something akin to "common sense," is the product of the moment in history into which they are born.

The corollary of that is that common sense, the benchmark of the human being, cannot be some preexisting constant, but must change through history. The subtitle of Foucault's book was *An Archaeology of the Human Sciences*. That refers to the Frenchman's suggestion that a modern human cannot hope to understand the thought processes of an ancient ancestor without first exploring the context in which they thought. Foucault went further to suggest that the entire concept of "mankind," or "human nature," was not one that our forebears would recognize. Instead it was an invention that dated back to the start of the 19th century (around the time of Immanuel Kant). This "invented" modern human, who is both an object to study and the means to study it, would be incomprehensible to both our ancestors and descendants who would think in different ways to us.

Foucault argued that every attempt to encapsulate human nature, such as Leonardo da Vinci's Vitruvian Man *from the 1490s, is only relevant to the time in which it was made.*

ARCHAEOLOGY OF THINKING

Michel Foucault proposed a new technique for figuring out how human nature has changed over the course of history. He called it the "archaeology of thinking," in which we need to dig up evidence of how people thought in the context of their own time. He proposed that it was possible to trace the history of ideas to form a kind of family tree—and suggested that the idea of human nature was just one of many branches that emerge from the past.

The bones of ancient humans resemble those of any modern descendants, but the content of their mind was very different.

85 The Trolley Problem

PHILIPPA FOOT, A BRITISH PHILOSOPHER, WAS INTERESTED IN VIRTUE ETHICS, THE IDEA THAT MORAL ACTS WERE THOSE THAT nurtured a good character, not those that maximized the common good. She illuminated this ancient idea with a modern thought experiment straight out of a B-movie thriller.

In 1967, Foot asked us to imagine ourselves in this simple scenario: You are standing in a signal box at a railroad junction. A runaway trolley is approaching, heading for five people tied to the track beneath you. On the track beside them is a single person tied in a similar manner but not in the path of the train. Within reach of you alone is the lever to divert the train onto a different track, saving the five bound unfortunates. However, that second track is the one where the single person is tied up. Do you pull the lever? Most of us agree that the best thing to do is pull the lever and switch the track, so one person dies but five are saved. This is a utilitarian approach: Pulling the lever results in the minimum harm to life and limb—but cannot prevent all harm.

Another scenario is that you are watching events from a footbridge above the track. This time the only way to save the five is to push a fat man standing next to you down onto the track. He would die, but derail the train and save the others. Most of us would not do this, perhaps because we become the primary cause of death, rather than an agent reducing the amount of death. Our desire to retain an untainted character makes killing the fat man seem immoral. However, if the fat man is recast as the villain who has tied the five to the rails in the first place, then the moral calculus is changed enough for us to give him a push over the edge.

Will she be saved out of virtue or just because it is the right thing to do?

86 Derrida's Deconstruction

JACQUES DERRIDA HAS BECOME THE ARCHETYPAL MODERN FRENCH PHILOSOPHER. HIS WORK IS DENSE AND AT TIMES BAFFLING because it attempts to analyze how words produce meaning—and he does that using words.

Is this Derrida? This text cannot say so.

Derrida achieved recognition in the world of philosophy for his 1967 book, *Of Grammatology*. Straight away we see that he used some very unwieldy terms to extend his ideas. "Grammatology" was in fact coined 15 years before by the Polish linguist Ignace Gelb, although Derrida would coin some of his own. It refers to the scientific study of writing systems. Derrida's central idea was that all texts are filled with contradictions, or *aporia*, a term he borrowed from the ancient Greeks (it means something like "confusion"). Derrida proposed a way of deconstructing text to whittle out these puzzles and show how words and meanings relate to one another.

Derrida suggests that we have been misinterpreting the power of language since the days before writing, when the spoken word had a "presence," or innate meaning, as the direct expression of the speaker's thoughts. And that concept was transferred to written text, despite writing being dislocated from the immediacy of speech.

Vive la différance

Derrida's next contribution is the idea of *différance*. His own mother is said to have pointed out that he'd spelled the word wrong, but that was intentional: The word is a French portmanteau of *différence* (difference) and *deférrer* (to defer). Différance is Derrida's method for explaining how the meaning of a text can never be known, not even by the author (don't ask me). The true meaning of each word is always deferred as it is further clarified with other words that follow it in the text. We may think we understand the point being made, and for all practical purposes that is enough. However, when it comes to philosophizing, then the process is infinitely long, or as Derrida put it: "Il n'y a pas de hors-texte." That translates directly to: "There is no outside text," but what Derrida means is all knowledge and experience are contained within the text, the meaning of which is deferred indefinitely. A quick example of *différance* would be: "Jacques Derrida ..." (a name of someone) ... "was a philosopher" (now we know who) ... "from France" ... (now we know more) ... "but he was not that famous one with the same name." At each deferment the meaning changes—but there is always more to say.

The word water *could refer to a large number of things. I could carry on clarifying what I mean by that one word but according to Derrida the true meaning requires an infinitely large text. I can only hope these pictures will give you a hint of what I am thinking.*

87 Quine and Words

IN 1968, WILLARD VAN ORMAN QUINE WAS WONDERING HOW WORDS HAVE ANY MEANING IN THE FIRST PLACE. By this time he was an elder statesman among American analytical philosophers with an interest in logical positivism, but he split from the pack by saying that words are meaningless.

Quine was a Harvard professor of long standing when he wrote his famous essay, *Ontological Relativity*. In it he discussed the problem of the "indeterminacy of translation." Put simply, he wanted to know how a word from one language could be translated into another exactly. How could you be sure that the translated word had the same meaning as the original one, and did not mean something slightly different (or completely different for that matter)? From that he surmised that instead of words being signifiers, or having a direct connection with objects or ideas, they were, in fact, only given meaning by the shared human skill of talking, or communicating with words. Quine summed this up by saying that language is a "social art."

Pegasus ridden by Perseus is many things to many people. In the end, the true meaning is something we can all agree on but no one really knows how.

Language experiment

Quine proposed a thought experiment, which we will refashion here to refer to Pegasus, the mythical horse, which had been a favorite subject of Quine's earlier in his career. Let's imagine we have no previous knowledge of ancient Greek cultures and we travel back in time to the mythical prehistory of Greek legends, when gods, heroes, and monsters were doing battle. We are on Mount Olympus visiting with Zeus when Pegasus arrives. Zeus (who we cannot understand at all) says "pegasus." We assume that the word means "winged horse." However, it could mean "white horse ridden by Perseus" or the "child of Poseidon and Medusa" or "Wow! That horse can fly, dude!" We can never know what the meaning of the word is—in fact it does not have one. This exchange reflects how we all learned to speak, by listening to the words other people say and then trying them out. Therefore, all words lack a definite meaning, and our ability to communicate with them comes down to an unspoken (ironically) agreement about what it all means.

"We do not learn first what to talk about and then what to say about it."

QUINE

88 Chomsky's Universal Rule

NOAM CHOMSKY IS RARE AMONG ACADEMIC FIGURES. HAVING SHIFTED THE PARADIGM OF LINGUISTICS IN THE 1950S, he then became better known as a political philosopher. In 1969, at the height of the counter-cultural movements in the West, he offered a rigorous method for questioning authority.

Amid the tumultuous cultural changes of the late 1960s, Noam Chomsky was not alone in noticing that what governments said they stood for in the world and what they actually did abroad did not match up. In the United States at the time this was largely against the backdrop of the Vietnam War, a conflict fought by America and other countries allied to South Vietnam against what was said to be an unjust, inhumane, and dangerous government in North Vietnam.

Chomsky was an opponent of America's intervention in that war, as set out in his 1969 book, *American Power and the New Mandarins*. However, he was making a wider philosophical point, that was irrespective of that opinion, right or wrong. He said that citizens of a state tend to assume that their rulers are more ethical than those of foreign governments, especially of those states which pose a threat or rivalry. However, said Chomsky, this is an illusion we choose to believe in and the end result of which is that ruling elites are able to behave unethically abroad in our name.

Satellite technology meant that near-live pictures of American forces in action in Vietnam were beamed into everyone's homes. In turn that led people to call into question the prosecution of the war. Specifically, Chomsky wondered whether Vietnam should benefit from the same standards applied in America.

Noam Chomsky put his linguistics career aside to become a prominent, often outspoken, political commentator, frequently questioning the foreign policies of successive U.S. governments in terms of the principles of universality.

Principle of universality

Chomsky's solution was the "principle of universality," an updating of the Golden Rule of ethics—you should treat others as you would like others to treat you—only applying it to governments. Citizens should constantly monitor what their government is doing by examining the facts, rather than listening to its announcements. When the government uses ethical reasons for acting against another foreign power, such as applying economic sanctions or taking military action, we are then able to compare "wrongs" of our enemy with the "rights" of own rulers. Only then can we be sure that the ethical arguments behind a policy are being applied universally.

89 Rawls's Veil of Ignorance

SINCE THE DAY OF HOBBES, THE IDEA OF THE SOCIAL CONTRACT WHERE INDIVIDUALS ACCEPT THE RESTRICTIONS OF LAWS IN RETURN for protection from each other has been well established. However, in 1971, an American philosopher revisited the way we ensure that laws are fair to all.

To be fair, justice must be blind to the original position of those involved so it can be delivered to all in equal measure.

John Rawls chose to be a professional philosopher after serving in World War II. As the conflict ended he witnessed the aftermath of the Hiroshima nuclear attack and was offered a promotion to an officer rank soon after. He rejected the idea, preferring to return to America and instead devote his life to the study of the nature of morality.

After more than 20 years in academe he published his most famous work, *The Theory of Justice,* in 1971. In it, he proposed a thought experiment that was meant to establish the fundamental principles of justice, which he defied any rational person to disagree with.

"The principles of justice are chosen behind a veil of ignorance."

RAWLS

Veil of ignorance

Rawls's thought experiment is set on a desert island where a group of strangers have become irrevocably marooned. There is no hope of rescue so they set about building a new society. To do that they must forge a social contract, that allows each individual to further their personal interests but also ensures all members of the new nation cooperate with each other.

The imaginary founding figures are all rational beings, and so there is no prospect of them agreeing crazy, superstitious rules, such as the first person to collect a bird's egg from a nearby island will choose the ruler for the next year (although that was how it was decided on Easter Island for a long time). By the same token the community will not agree rules that favor one person (or a minority) over the rest, such as ginger-haired people are always served twice as much food. So how does the group, with its competing personal interests, find a system acceptable to all? Rawls said that can only be achieved by using a "veil of ignorance." He asks us to imagine that we are yet to be born and are entirely ignorant of the situation of our birth—rich or poor, etc. Only once we are freed from preconceived ideas of what is beneficial to our particular situation can we formulate a system that is most fair. Rawls's "veil" encourages us to "maximize the minimum" standards in society.

90 Animal Rights

IN 1975, THE AUSTRALIAN PHILOSOPHER PETER SINGER APPLIED UTILITARIAN ETHICS IN A NEW WAY. Jeremy Bentham's system was devoted to maximizing pleasure and minimizing pain. Singer was interested in how that impacted on all suffering—even the pain experienced by animals.

The system of ethics set out by Jeremy Bentham at the tail end of the 18th century is based on the consequences of acts (rather than the virtue of the actor). It is reduced to a simple equation: Moral acts are those in which the pleasure produced outweighs the pain. Every person impacted by an act is treated equally, or as Bentham put it: "Each to count for one, and none for more than one." Singer's 1975 book, *Animal Liberation,* looks at the utilitarian equation again, but takes into account pain in nonhumans. His new question was: What value does an animal's pain carry in the calculations?

Pain is both a mechanistic signal from the body that damage has occurred, and a perception akin to seeing an image or hearing a sound. Therefore, while one person's pain is theirs alone, Singer argues that all pain is the same—if it is felt by a dog, frog, or human being. However, he does add the caveat that the extent to which a frog, for example, can feel pain compared to a human is unclear. Nevertheless, his central point is that to act without taking into account pain caused in nonhuman animals is immoral. That calls into question the morality of a meat diet, since that requires killing many animals to feed each person. However, medical experiments that cause pain in a few animals in order to lessen suffering in many humans is entirely moral within Singer's ethical framework.

Advocates for animal rights protest against the pet trade. According to Singer's ethics, caging intelligent animals as pets is immoral.

91 Mentalese: The Language of Thought

IN 1975, AMERICAN JERRY FODOR SUGGESTED AN ANSWER TO THE PUZZLE OF HOW WE LEARN TO use language to express ideas. His idea was that we are all born fluent in (although are never able to speak) the same language.

Fodor's Mentalese is a language without any words, just ideas arranged in a logical order.

Fodor's Mentalese was not just a proforma that allowed us to learn a natural language—one that involves making sounds—but was the language used to think with throughout our lives. Now you're thinking, "But I think in English" (or whatever language is your mother tongue). Fodor's response was that the Mentalese thought preceded this one, and was translated into natural language as your brain formulated what to say. This process is already at work in a newborn, before they have acquired their natural language. This explains how, according to Fodor, we can learn to verbalize our ideas despite, as Quine had found a few years before, individual words being inherently meaningless.

The Mentalese "words" follow the same rules as a natural language. However, they are not heard or represented like the words of another language. Instead, elementary concepts are assembled in logical order to form the thought. For example, the idea "my brain is spinning" requires three components: Brain; the idea of something being mine (not yours); and spin or rotate. When these Mentalese units combine we have that whole idea. Fodor often referred to mental activity as involving computational thought, akin to Turing's "thinking machine." In some respects, Mentalese is like the machine code of a computer which receives an input and calculates the answer before giving the output—the conscious thought. It can all occur very quickly but has a specific order. The latest neuroscience has added a new component to this idea: In 2008, it was found that conscious thoughts arise about half a second after their associated mental activity. Maybe that is the time we take to talk to ourselves in Mentalese?

"If there is a community of computers living in my head, there had also better be somebody who is in charge; and, by God, it had better be me." FODOR

92 Memetics

ALTHOUGH PERHAPS NOT AN ENTIRE PHILOSOPHY IN ITSELF, MEMETICS NEVERTHELESS SEEKS TO SHED LIGHT ON HOW SOME IDEAS persist while others are forgotten. Whether the very idea of memetics will persist remains to be seen, although it has been growing in strength since its inception in 1976.

Memetics is the brainchild of the British evolutionary biologist, Richard Dawkins. He proposed it as something of a digression in his 1976 breakthrough book, *The Selfish Gene*. That book was a popular retelling of neo-Darwinism, which recasts the theory of evolution by natural selection at the level of genes rather than individuals. The term "gene" has several definitions, but one that Dawkins uses is "the unit of inheritance." In other words, genes are the things that are passed from parents to offspring, and which make us similar to our relatives.

Like all intellectuals, Richard Dawkins is interested in spreading his memes as widely as possible.

In accordance with the theory of evolution, genes are in competition to be inherited. Some succeed and spread into more and more families with each generation while others fail and eventually die—or become extinct. By way of illustration of this, the book's central point, Dawkins then proposed that genes are not the only things that behave in this kind of way: Ideas do it as well. He coined the word *meme* to describe a unit analogous to a gene, and so memetics is also analogous to genetics.

Meme was derived from the Greek word for "to copy." A meme is an idea that contains within it the need to pass it on. It could be a joke, a skill, or a philosophy. If it is a good idea—funny, useful, or enlightening—the second person will pass it on. As it spreads it may change slightly, or mutate, during transmission. Mutant versions can supersede the original, or they may fail, and like their counterparts in genetics, become extinct.

INTERNET MEMES

To be successful, a meme must be communicated to as many people as possible, and there is nothing better than the Internet for that. Internet memes are frequently pointless crazes. They grow at a huge rate and then die away almost as fast.

The Harlem Shake meme saw people performing a specific dance in increasingly absurd locations.

93 Midgley on Culture

IN HER 1978 BOOK, *BEAST AND MEN*, THE ENGLISH MORAL PHILOSOPHER MARY MIDGLEY ARGUED AGAINST reducing human nature to a biological process. To her this was not the only way to understand ourselves. In fact, she argued, even the most modern motivations of human life are just as natural as any primitive urge.

Central to Midgley's work is the idea that human beings are somehow separate from nature. This idea, that has been compounded over the years in different philosophies, emphasizes how human beings have a unique consciousness, a viewpoint from which to observe reality that is not available to other animals. On top of that, many philosophers consider human nature to be the complex product of a jumble of cultural influences, the composition of which varies through time, and which acts to modify our primitive "natural" selves.

Culture is natural

Learned culture is not solely a human feature. These snow monkeys keep warm in winter by bathing in a volcanic spring. This behavior is not universal to the species, but is a cultural feature of a group that lives in a nature park in Japan.

Midgley rejected the idea that culture was somehow artificial, and that revealing the truth about humanity meant reducing it to its simplest parts—such as anatomy and genetics. She argued that this was just one way of describing ourselves and there are "many windows" through which to look at ourselves. In contrast with the traditions of earlier philosophers, she points out that cultures are not unique to human societies—we now know that primates, dolphins, and even crows pass on learned behaviors to new generations—and culture itself should be regarded as just as essential a part of our natural state as our genes or biochemistry.

94 The Postmodern Condition

IN 1979, THE WORD *MODERN* BECAME OLD-FASHIONED. **THE FRENCH PHILOSOPHER JEAN-FRANÇOIS LYOTARD** heralded the end of the modern era, saying that knowledge was now being divorced from the mind and was becoming a commodity to be bought and sold.

We rely on computers to do the remembering for us in the modern world.

We live in the Postmodern age. So what's changed? The Modern society had thrown out superstition and was built on reason and evidence, and a Modern person was improved by accruing knowledge. In Lyotard's 1979 book, *The Postmodern Condition: A Report into Knowledge*, the Frenchman summed up what he thought set the Postmodern person apart from his or her Modern forebears: "an incredulity toward meta-narratives." Perhaps not the most pithy phrase once translated from French, but his point was that we were becoming less convinced that reason was going to be able to sum up the human condition with a simple explanation (a meta-narrative) that covered all the complexities of life. For example, a dominant meta-narrative of that period was Marxism, which was increasingly being shown to be limited in its effectiveness.

Knowledge shift

The result was a shift in people's attitude toward knowledge. No longer was knowledge something contained inside a person's head. This was the dawn of the computer age, and knowledge of all kinds was being stored as data in the external world. Computer data is highly transferable and, therefore, knowledge about the world was becoming a commodity that could be sold. The value of knowing something had become monetary, not philosophical.

FUTURE SHOCK

In 1970, Alvin Toffler (right) discussed the consequences of our ability to collect more and more information about the world in his book *Future Shock*. He suggested that as this trend was set to continue, we would become increasingly confused by the speed at which our understanding of the world changed. However, his worst fears have yet to be realized. In the postmodern world, humans do not need to "know" all the data—we leave computers to do it.

Gaia: Science or Religion?

THE GAIA HYPOTHESIS IS ONE OF A VERY FEW FIELDS OF ENDEAVOR THAT IS CLAIMED AS THEIR OWN BY MANY DISPARATE SCHOOLS OF THOUGHT. To some it is a philosophy, others give it a spiritual dimension, while its originator meant it as a means to understand nature.

> *"Life does more than adapt to the Earth. It changes the Earth to its own purposes."*
>
> LOVELOCK

The Gaia Hypothesis was developed in the 1970s and set out in a 1979 book by the English scientist, James Lovelock. Lovelock was something of a maverick. After years working in industry and in academia he struck out on his own, building a laboratory inside his home and becoming that rare breed, an independent scientist and inventor. It was not that he had lacked impact while working for institutions: He performed some of the early research into CFCs, the ozone-depleting gases that have since been banned, and he worked at NASA on the *Viking* program, developing ways in which spacecraft could detect any signs of life after landing on Mars. While pondering how to do this, Lovelock began to consider what it was about Earth on the grand scale that showed evidence of its life. This work gave him a new way of looking at how Earth's biosphere—the narrow region around Earth's surface where life exists—might be operating.

The living planet

Lovelock's idea was eventually encapsulated as the Gaia Hypothesis. This states that planet Earth acts as a single, self-regulatory unit made up of the myriad interactions between living things and inanimate, abiotic things like the air, sea, and soil. Just as

DAISY WORLD

Lovelock illustrated Gaia using a primitive 1980s, computer simulation called Daisyworld. Dasiyworld had only two life-forms: White daisies reflected the Sun's heat, while black daisies absorbed it. The simulation showed that the proportions of white and black daisies oscillated along with a rise and fall of global temperature. A large number of white daisies made the planet cool, making it easier for black daisies to grow (they hang on to heat better). As the number of black daisies rose, the planet warmed, making it more likely that white flowers thrived, since they shed unneeded heat better—and the process repeated.

a living body—like yours—is able to regulate its conditions, such as its temperature, hydration, and sugar levels, within the narrow range required to keep it alive, Lovelock proposed that Earth did the same. For example, in his NASA days, Lovelock had noticed that Earth's atmosphere was very unstable with the proportions of its gases in constant flux—most unlike what we have since learned about Mars or other planets. However, the fluctuations remain in a very narrow range—and by and large have not varied far from that range over much of Earth's history. Lovelock found similar stability in ocean salinity and global temperatures, but the mechanisms he proposed for how they were regulated are hard to verify. One suggestion was that a rise in oxygen levels in the atmosphere would result in more fires, which would lead to a reduction in the amount of oxygen. Nevertheless, the idea that complex system of Earth was self-regulating like a living body was a compelling one to many.

Mixed reaction

Lovelock's theory does not overturn any earlier theories, such as Darwinism, but seeks to extend them. However, it was not well received by the scientific community, but in contrast was welcomed by environmentalists and the "new-age" counterculture who relished the idea that Earth was a living entity in its own right. In recent years, Lovelock has suggested that these responses were down to the choice of the name for his ideas: Gaia is the Greek goddess of Earth. (The name Gaia was actually proposed by Lovelock's friend the author William Golding, who is most famous for writing *Lord of The Flies*, an allegory of the many conflicting urges that underlie the social contract.)

The idea that the whole of Earth's surface operates as a single unit has inspired people in different ways. After decades of criticism, many of Lovelock's ideas are now being used by climate modelers and ecologists who study the impacts of human activities on "natural" processes.

Scientific criticisms were leveled at the methods and language Lovelock used, which he addressed in later work in collaboration with Lyn Margulis, an American biologist, but scientists continued to suspect that Lovelock was proposing that Earth as a whole constituted a higher form of life, a superorganism of some sort. Although Lovelock has been circumspect about this claim—his hypothesis suggests that the planet shares similar characteristics to an organism—it was this idea that appealed so much to many who saw it as a scientific validation of Earth-inspired spiritualism.

Gaian philosophy is a broad church that draws on ideas from Rousseau, Schlegel, and Eastern philosophies. Its adherents argue that modern civilization is disrupting the balance of Earth, and we should act to ensure the planet can regulate itself. Lovelock is not necessarily one of them—he recently advocated the use of nuclear power as a way of solving climate change. And if humanity persists in being an unstable influence on the biosphere, Gaian theory would suggest that humanity itself will be regulated

James Lovelock's laboratory is inside his home in western England and is not part of a university or corporation.

96 Personal Identity

IN HIS 1984 BOOK, *REASONS AND PERSONS*, THE BRITISH PHILOSOPHER DEREK PARFIT UPDATED OUR VIEW OF JOHN LOCKE'S analysis of identity. Where Locke proposed a mind and memory swap between a prince and a pauper, Parfitt teleports himself to Mars in his thought experiment.

If our physical body could be teleported to a new location, would our identity travel with it?

Like John Locke before him, Parfit wanted to know if a person's identity is based on the body or the mind. Locke had argued that a person's mental world, that which gave them their self-identity, was entirely the product of their experiences. Since this was a cumulative process in which new experiences modified our desires and beliefs, that meant our identity was always changing. The question remained: What links these different identities to create a person? Is it the association with the body or is it the fact that we have memories of the times when our accumulated experiences—and identities—were different?

Mind or body

Locke had imagined the mind of a prince being transferred to a pauper's body. That told him that personal identity is not linked to the body: The prince would still remember his majestic life and still regard himself as royal. Parfit decided to inject a bit of 20th-century thinking into the problem. He imagined a teleportation device that converted the physical body into data and then used that data to rematerialize the exact same body somewhere else—like Mars. But the machine goes wrong and two versions of the Martian explorer appear on the planet. Do they both have the same identity, or are they two different people?

Both share the memories of the original explorer and have equal claim to his identity, but from the moment of their materialization they have lived separate lives and are, therefore, no longer identical. Parfit sees this as evidence that identity only exists in the present and is not dependent on the body's survival. Any sense of identity linking back into the past is a product of a more dominant yearning to survive into the future, and to do that creates a feeling of continuity with the past.

"My life seemed like a glass tunnel, at the end of which there was darkness. When I changed my view, the walls of my glass tunnel disappeared. I now live in the open air."

PARFIT

97 Sage Philosophy

WESTERN TRADITIONS DOMINATE THE WORLD OF PHILOSOPHY BECAUSE THEY HAVE COMMUNICATED MORE SUCCESSFULLY OVER THE MILLENNIA, but does that make them more correct than the ideas from other cultures?

Our story of philosophy began with what we know from the writings of ancient Greeks, and what later people wrote in response. Similarly, the ideas of Eastern thought are known to us because they were written. But that means all those ideas that were never written down are being ignored. As a result, the field of philosophy is biased toward a few cultures that have their genesis in the Mediterranean region, Mesopotamia, the Indus Valley, and central China—and chiefly the former.

Oral traditions

Some have argued that cultures without a writing system have nothing to offer philosophy at large. However, the Kenyan philosopher Henry Odera Oruka disagreed. He set about recording the attitudes of Kenya's various traditional tribal cultures toward a wide range of philosophical themes, such as the nature of God and what is meant by freedom and justice.

Shamanism is where priests enter an altered state of consciousness using fasting or hallucinogens to divine wisdom. Oruka differentiated this idea of wisdom from sage philosophy.

To do this he observed everyday life in villages to establish a cultural context and then interviewed the members of the community considered the most wise, challenging them to back up their "wise" claims. He found that elders and priests often had a rational basis for their belief systems, which could be regarded as the equal of established forms of philosophy, past and present. Oruka spent more than 20 years collecting his data and published it in a book titled *Sage Philosophy* in 1994. The term "sage philosophy" refers to the combined body of a traditional belief system that is transmitted from generation to generation.

A traditional Masai gathering is an opportunity to see sage philosophy at work.

98 Philosophical Zombies

HOW DO YOU KNOW THAT YOU ARE NOT THE SOLE SURVIVOR OF A ZOMBIE INVASION? EVERYONE AROUND YOU BEHAVES PERFECTLY NORMALLY, INTERACTING WITH you as if they have a mind like yours. However, what evidence is there that they are not mindless—in other words, zombies?

This was an idea that the Australian philosopher David Chalmers asked us to grapple with in 1996. In so doing he was exploring the field of dualism, as proposed by Avicenna and Descartes centuries before. Dualism suggests that the mind and body are two separate things. If dualism is the true state of a conscious being, then Chalmers suggested that a philosophical zombie, which is all body and no mind, is possible.

Deceptive appearance

One of the central tenets of dualism is that the neither the body nor the mind can be reduced into being a part of the other one. So any clues that a person has a mind is only available through the behavior of their body. But even if a zombie behaves as if it has a mind, it doesn't mean it has one.

Imagine you are walking down the street and you bump into another person, as bad luck would have it treading on each other's feet and knocking heads together. You shout "Ow!" and hop around rubbing your sore head and foot to soothe the pain you feel. The other person does the same. Does that mean they are feeling pain like you? What evidence is there that they are not a zombie just following an instinctive or preprogrammed response?

Take a close look at these Quentin Tarantinos. Which one is the philosophical zombie?

Hard problem

Chalmers uses this idea to address the hard problem of consciousness. The "easy" problems are to do with people expressing their conscious thoughts, reporting the content of their mind. However, the hard problem is to do with how we can imagine things beyond our experience and the sensations we have that are linked with consciousness, like color or smells. Philosophers call these internal feelings "qualia." Where do they come from? Chalmers suggests that since it is possible to have a physical zombie twin who is identical in every way, except lacking qualia, then the mind itself must be nonphysical.

99 The Postphilosophical Society

BY THE LATE 1990s, RICHARD RORTY WAS ARGUING that philosophy could not reveal any absolute truth about the best way to live. Instead, society was always questioning what was right and wrong.

When faced with a tricky ethical question that is open to debate, we often choose our position by resorting simply to how we feel about it. We just "feel" it is wrong or right. (We might "feel" it in our bones, or our heart "tells" us, or we just "know" but don't know why.) It is perhaps surprising that in our age of rationalism and advanced analysis we still end up making ethical decisions in this way. Does this imply that we have some deep, unexamined connection with a natural goodness that is external to us? Throughout his career, the American pragmatist philosopher Richard Rorty offered an alternative view: We set our moral compass ourselves. Wrong and right are our own inventions, and have changed over human history.

RELATIVE MORALS

The postphilosophical world, said Richard Rorty, is one without moral absolutes. The morality of a society develops though the solidarity of its members. Every moral question remains open to debate, and if enough people protest against something, then it is eventually agreed to be wrong. What is "good" is constantly being redefined by this active process. To live in a moral society does not mean that we must accept fixed rules but requires everyone to engage in the ongoing debate.

Protesters dress as embryos in a demonstration against medical research into human stem cells. The rights and wrongs of this new field are still being debated.

Mirror mind

Rorty proposed that the feeling that we have some primordial link to a natural morality comes from a misconception of what our view of the world tells us. He disputed that our senses mirror reality in a machine process, where raw data is collected by the senses and then combined to present a full picture of our surroundings. Instead, our perceptions are also reflecting our customs and beliefs about the world, and this is what creates a false intuition that external reality is able to inform us about ethical questions. So what's the result of this philosophy? Rorty proposes that morality is entirely invented and what is wrong and right are subject to agreement with other people. In short, you are behaving morally as long as other members of society agree that you can get away with it. Socrates said very much the same thing 2,500 years ago!

Rorty argued that our mind's eye is not like the screen of a camera—it does not collect and restructure information from the outside world. Instead, our cultural customs and beliefs mold our perceptions as well, so our view of the world is biased toward them and is not a simple representation of reality.

100 Is This a Computer Simulation?

DURING THE LAST TEN YEARS, PHILOSOPHY HAS TURNED TO THE COMPUTER AS A WAY OF UNDERSTANDING WHAT IT IS TO BE HUMAN. Nick Bostrom, a Swedish philosopher, has proposed that the chances are that our Universe—and all of us—exists inside a computer from the future!

Moore's law is based on a prediction made by Gordon Moore, the founder of microchip manufacturers Intel, in 1965. He said that computer power would double roughly every 18 months, and he was proved right, more or less, although the rate of increase has slowed in recent years. Nevertheless, computer-processing power today is gargantuan compared to the 1960s and it is easy to imagine it growing ever bigger in future. Bostrom has suggested that at some point computing technology—both the hardware and software—would become so powerful, that it would give a future culture the ability to manipulate all matter and simulate any natural process. He calls this state "technological maturity" and any civilization that reaches this level of development has unlimited possibilities.

"There could be many more simulated people than non-simulated people."

BOSTROM

What next?
Bostrom's Simulation Argument focuses on one activity in a technologically mature culture—ancestry simulation. This is a

ARTIFICIAL INTELLIGENCE
Computers can perform many more tasks per second than the humble human brain, but can they think? Thinking is not about going through every possible permutation of a problem until you find the right one. A computer can do that but it would take an almost infinitely long time. The thinking human succeeds where the computer fails by knowing what to ignore and how to focus in on the most likely solutions. This is called "heuristics" and computer scientists are trying to program it into computers. If they succeed, what would separate a human thought from one inside a computer?

computational experiment, where our future selves attempt to understand how we, their ancestors, lived by running simulations of the past. Today's scientists might be doing something similar, modeling the weather or stock markets in an attempt to understand them better. However, a mature civilization could recreate an entire Universe so exactly it would be very hard to tell the real one from the simulated versions.

Three possibilities

Bostrom analyzed this idea to find out if it was at all likely that simulations existed. His approach had three parts. First he considered the likelihood of a civilization reaching technological maturity. Perhaps it was impossible—the time required is so long that a solar system was always destroyed before maturity was reached. Perhaps the process of developing the technology was so fraught with danger that civilizations invariably destroyed themselves as they did so, through wars or accidents. However, Bostrom concluded that it was plausible that a small, "non-negligible" number of civilizations could reach maturity.

Next he considered whether a mature civilization would be interested in running ancestry simulations. Perhaps in the course of maturation they would have achieved a good understanding of the past or would not find further knowledge of it useful in any way. If so, they won't bother devoting their efforts to simulate a universe. However, perhaps there are other reasons to do so—maybe simulated universes are a source of entertainment, like games or even pets. So, again Bostrom concludes that even though it could be a minority of them, some mature civilizations would perform ancestry simulation.

Finally then, he concludes that it is more likely than not that you and everyone else is a simulated being existing inside a computer from the future. His reasoning is that even though the chance of a mature civilization with a desire to simulate its past is very low, once it did so it would be capable of producing an astronomically high number of simulations. As a result there are far more realities that are computer simulated than are not.

In 2012, astronomers began to look for a way of checking if our Universe is a simulation. The latest theory suggests that a simulation would have to define limits to matter and energy, and the place to look for them is in the ultrahigh energy cosmic rays that permeate the Universe. What will we do if it turns out we are all in fact computer characters?

In the 1999 movie, The Matrix, *characters realize that reality is a simulation and so find they can take on superhuman powers. However, the rules of a simulated universe are just as unbreakable as the laws of "real" physics.*

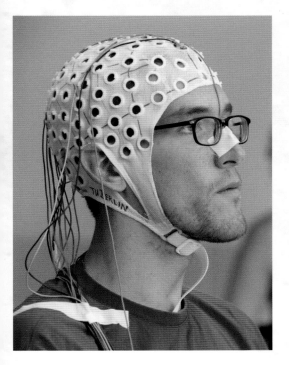

New scanning techniques are being used to map the functions of our brain, but humans are currently not clever enough to understand the human brain. There are more connections in it than there are star systems in the Universe. Even if we could one day simulate a Universe, is simulating a brain much harder?

CYBER SELF

In a small way, part of our identity already exists inside computers. Social media and search services collect so much data about our behavior that they create a unique individual that exists online. Perhaps in technologically mature societies consciousness will have transferred from the body or brain to computers.

Schools of Philosophy

SOMETIMES KNOWN AS SCHOOLS, ALSO KNOWN AS MOVEMENTS OR APPROACHES, EVERY PHILOSOPHER'S WORK BELONGS TO AT LEAST ONE OF THESE CHARACTERISTIC GROUPS. ALL PHILOSOPHERS TRY TO PRODUCE WORK THAT GOES BEYOND THE CONTENT OF A SCHOOL, MOST FAIL, but a few of them achieve an outlook so new and pristine that it becomes the founder work of a new school.

There are many ways of classifying, dividing up, and organizing the fields of philosophy. At the largest scale, we talk about its branches. Philosophy has many aims, and we have presented five here, each of which can be distilled into a field of endeavor:

METAPHYSICS, the study of existence aims to discover the nature of reality.

EPISTEMOLOGY, the study of knowledge tries to reveal the nature of truth and how we can know things.

ETHICS is the philosophy of right and wrong, which aims to understand how we can live well and can say something is good and bad.

POLITICS is the study of power, which is the study of the good society, proposing the systems by which groups of people can live together.

AESTHETICS is the study of art and attempts to figure out the nature of beauty and how this informs our view of the world.

Each branch asks a big question, and all schools of philosophy are suggesting a means to answer them. There are dozens of philosophical schools. Many of them are relics of the past, while the modern ones are often closely allied to other fields, such as psychology, mathematics, and economics. Let's take a look at a few of the main schools.

Solipsism

A solipsist does not differentiate between the objective reality of the world and the subjective reality of our imagination. Solipsism says they are both the same thing, with the objective being a subset of the subjective. Therefore, the only thing you can know to exist is your own existence. Everyone and everything else can only be proven to be the product of your mind, and the content of your mind is entirely distinct from the content of another person's mind—if they even exist!

Leading figures:	René Descartes, George Berkeley
Major works:	*Principles of Philosophy*, Descartes, 1644; *A Treatise Concerning the Principles of Human Knowledge*, Berkeley, 1710

? Would the last person on Earth be a solipsist?

'*When a solipsist dies ... everything goes with him.*'

DAVID FOSTER WALLACE

Determinism

This school of thought maintains that every event past, present, and future is already defined, the direct product of a past cause having a future effect. So a star exploding, atoms reacting, and a person thinking are all part of a grand orchestrated reality . Determinists need not agree how the reality was set in train—or by whom. It could be God or a set of physical laws, or both. Compatibilists propose a soft determinism in which free will is still possible in a determined Universe.

Leading figures:	Heraclitus, Boëthius, Baruch Spinoza, Pierre-Simon Laplace, Moses Maimonides
Major works:	*Consolation of Philosophy*, Boëthius, 524 CE

? If the future is set can we have free will?

'*A man can do what he wants, but not want what he wants.*'

ARTHUR SCHOPENHAUER

Utilitarianism

This is a branch of ethics, which states that the moral worth of an action is determined by how much it contributes to the common good, or overall utility. The crucial aspect of an action is its consequence, or outcome. At its most basic, all that matters is the effect of your actions, not really what you do. Put simply, the ends justify the means. There are two approaches: Society can define behaviors to maximize utility or punish harmful behaviors that have no utility.

Leading figures:	Niccolò Machiavelli, Jeremy Bentham, John Stuart Mill
Major works:	*On Liberty*, Mill, 1859; *Introduction to Principles of Morals and Legislation*, Bentham, 1780; *The Prince*, Machiavelli, 1532

? Is it allowed to do anything as long as it does no harm to others?

'*The end justifies the means as long as there is something that justifies the end.*'

LEON TROTSKY

Epicureanism

Named for Epicurus, this philosophy proposes that the purpose of existence is to seek pleasure, here and now. This is in opposition to religious teachings that demand we defer pleasure to a later point (generally after death) and endure pain and suffering in order to achieve it. True Epicureans are not just seeking sex and food and fun. They also achieve pleasure by obtaining knowledge, through friendship, and living a virtuous life—in other words, helping others find pleasure. This modifies it against hedonism, where physical pleasure is the goal.

Leading figures:	Epicurus, Lucretius, Jeremy Bentham, Thomas Jefferson
Major works:	*Lives of Eminent Philosophers*, Diogenes Laertius, 250 BCE

? Is life without pain possible?

' "Carpe diem!" Seize the day'
HORACE

Positivism

This philosophy only accepts knowledge that is true by definition or has been proven by a strict scientific investigation—in other words, arises from a positive affirmation of a theory. Positivism is closely linked to empiricism. Truth by definition reveals only trivial (i.e. insignificant) facts, while nontrivial knowledge is based on our sensory experiences rather than intellectual reasoning alone. Logical positivists focus on the language used to express knowledge to ensure it does not mislead.

Leading figures:	A.J. Ayer, Rudolf Carnap
Major works:	*Language, Truth, and Logic*, Ayer, 1936 *Philosophy and Logical Syntax*, Carnap, 1935

? Is it possible to verify a truth beyond doubt through experience, or does the experience just make the truth more probable?

'It is man's unique privilege, among all other organisms. By pursuing falsehood you will arrive at the truth!'
FYODOR DOSTOYEVSKY

Absurdism

An absurdist proclaims that the search for the meaning of life will end in failure since there is no meaning to our existence, and the absurdity is that we value our lives more than anything. While a nihilist responds to the meaningless life by believing nothing, an absurdist finds meaning in actions—while (absurdly) accepting they are fundamentally meaningless.

Leading figures:	Albert Camus
Major works:	*L'Étranger (The Stranger)*, Camus, 1942; *Le Mythe de Sisyphe (The Myth of Sisyphus)*, Camus, 1942

? Should we acknowledge meaninglessness or construct a meaning?

'Freedom is nothing but a chance to be better.'
CAMUS

Objectivism

This relatively modern school of philosophy was introduced by Ayn Rand in the 1960s. It states that reality is entirely objective and independent of the mind. The mind connects with reality through the senses and all rationality flows from that by the choices a person makes. Therefore, rationality is personal and individual and so social systems can only work if they allow for members of society to behave as individuals acting in their own self-interest.

Leading figures: Ayn Rand

Major works: *The Fountainhead*, Rand, 1943; *Atlas Shrugged*, Rand, 1957

? Is being selfish more moral than being selfless?

'Do not confuse altruism with kindness, good will, or respect for the rights of others.'

AYN RAND

Humanism

Truth and morality are wholly in the hands of humanity, not handed down as absolutes by a divine being. So say secular humanists. Therefore, the good life is also a human construction. "Do as you would have others do to you," is the "Golden Rule" of secularism. Instead of religious rules or threats, humanists rely on reason and empathy for ethical decisions. The first humanists were actually very religious—including Martin Luther, the force behind the Protestant Reformation—and for them humanism was to elevate the consideration of human nature, art, and literature (the so-called humanities) to the same level as religion and classical philosophy.

Leading figures: Desiderius Erasmus, Martin Luther

Major works: *The Praise of Folly*, Erasmus, 1511

? Did humanism exist before humans?

'Being a humanist means trying to behave decently without expectation of rewards or punishment after you are dead.'

KURT VONNEGUT

Nihilism

Is this a philosophy at all? A nihilist doesn't care. It's all pointless. Nihilism rejects the very concepts that philosophers have spilt so much ink over for millennia: Truth does not matter; nothing can be good or bad; God never existed; and the Universe is meaningless. Nihilists may sound like sad, lonely pessimists, and that's because some of them are, but the school has inspired a lot of modern art, such as surrealism and the Dada movement.

Leading figures: Søren Kierkegaard, Friedrich Nietzsche, Martin Heidegger, Jean-François Lyotard

Major works: *Fathers and Sons*, Ivan Turgenev, 1862

? If nothing matters, why does nihilism?

'Nothing exists; even if something exists, nothing can be known about it; and even if something can be known about it, knowledge about it can't be communicated to others.'

GORGIAS

Existentialism

Not known for its chuckles, existentialism is the study of how we are born, live, and die alone. To an existentialist everything begins with the person. Their existence precedes thoughts, feelings, and ethics. As a result an existentialist creates a separation between the self and the rest of the Universe, leading to an angsty, absurd, even desperate outlook, but an authentic one.

Leading figures:	Søren Kierkegaard, Friedrich Nietzsche, Jean-Paul Sartre, Simone de Beauvoir
Major works:	*Fear and Trembling*, Kierkegaard, 1843; *Thus Spake Zarathrustra*, Nietzsche, 1885; *Nausea*, Satre 1938

? Who decides?

'Try again. Fail again. Fail better.'

SAMUEL BECKETT

Neoplatonism

A reworking of Plato's philosophy that rose to the fore in the latter stages of the Roman Empire. By that time, the original Greek philosophy was being infused with mysticism from the Middle East and that resulted in a philosophy that merges monotheism (there is only one God) with monism (the source of being has one source). As in Judaism, the neoplatonists did not talk of evil, just the absence of good. The hierarchy of the Universe (starting with the One) in some ways mirrors the Holy Trinity, although the Christian creed, as we understand it today, came later.

Leading figures:	Plotinus, Hypatia, Proclus, Avicenna
Major works:	*The Six Enneads*, Plotinus, c.270 CE

'The soul exists partly in eternity and partly in time.'

MARSILIO FICINO

Stoicism

The term "stoic" is still in common usage: It means someone who bears suffering without complaining. The Stoic school of philosophy was at its height in the centuries either side of the life of Jesus. Stoics sought to control their emotions and desires in order to devote themselves to reason—seen as the superior facet of humanity. Stoic philosophers had an unusually good turn of phrase: "Virtue is nothing else than right reason," said Seneca the Younger. In many ways Stoicism was the opposite path to Epicureanism, although both believed the truth about the world was something that people could discover.

Leading figures:	Zeno of Citium, Seneca the Younger, Epictetus
Major works:	*Meditations*, Marcus Aurelius, 180 CE

? Which is best, the quality of life or the quantity?

'Freedom is secured not by the fulfilling of men's desires, but by the removal of desire.'

EPICTETUS

Skepticism

"I know one thing: That I know nothing." So said Socrates, the founding father of skepticism, which refutes all knowledge. To a skeptic from the Classical era, knowledge is impossible. That created a bit of a roadblock for this school, and it was not until the 16th century that the philosophy of skepticism began to move forward, with the work of Michel de Montaigne. Rather than refute everything anyone said, as Socrates did, Montaigne is dubbed a skeptic because he sought to cut through the emotional content of an argument to reveal the hard, reasoned truths.

Leading figures:	Socrates, Pyrrho, Michel de Montaigne, David Hume
Major works:	*Essays*, Montaigne, 1580

? Is skepticism useful?

'It is evident that skepticism, while it makes no actual change in man, always makes him feel better.'

AMBROSE BIERCE

Idealism

This school of philosophy purports that the truth about the world resides in the mind. Any empirical evidence of the true and possible reality you might think you collect all has to be done using the mind and, therefore, is as much a mental construction as imagining something impossible and unreal. As it stands, the most radical modern philosophy—that the Universe is an artificial model in some huge computer—is a form of idealism. It's just in someone, or something, else's mind, not yours.

Leading figures:	George Berkeley, Immanuel Kant, Georg Hegel
Major works:	*The Praise of Folly*, Erasmsus, 1511

? Can knowledge be revealed through thought alone?

'An idealist is one who, on noticing that a rose smells better than a cabbage, concludes that it makes a better soup.'

BERTRAND RUSSELL

Structuralism

Put simply, this means that human understanding is formed on the basis of some larger, all-pervading structure. The events of the world occur within that structure and we perceive them in a way defined by that structure. The term *structure* is generally applied to mean the interrelations of words and their meanings and the framework of cultural taboos and traditions, rather than physical laws. Deconstruction, developed by Jacques Derrida, is a modern field related to structuralism.

Leading figures:	Ferdinand de Saussure, Claude Lévi-Strauss, Jacques Derrida
Major works:	*La Pensée Sauvage*, Lévi-Strauss, 1962

? Does everything happen for a reason?

'Deconstruction insists not that truth is illusory but that it is institutional.'

TERRY EAGLETON

Phenomenology

The phenomenon in phenomenology has a specific definition. A "phenomenon" is the name for what we perceive in our mind, a mental picture or construct. The real object that is being perceived to engender that phenomenon is termed the "noumenon." A noumenon is an entity outside the mind which we can only perceive as a "phenomenon." So phenomenology is the philosophy that tackles the subjective content of our consciousness, such as emotions and judgment, without resorting to noumea to explain them. In addition, in order to describe the noumea, we must employ *a priori* concepts such as space and time, which belong to the phenomenal world.

Leading figures: Georg Hegel, Immanuel Kant, Edmund Husserl, Martin Heidegger

Major works: *Critique of Pure Reason*, Kant, 1781; *Experience and Judgment*, Husserl, 1939

? What is the mind made of?

'The body is our general medium for having a world.'

MAURICE MERLEAU-PONTY

Empiricism

The opposite of rationalism (*see* below), this school of thought says that all knowledge can only be acquired through the senses. The musings of the mind can only reveal truths if they are based on evidence received from the outside world. A mind without the ability to sense the outside world, an empiricist insists, knows nothing and is empty of thoughts. Any ideas a mind does have can only be true once they are verified with evidence or tested through experience.

Leading figures: Aristotle, John Locke, David Hume, John Stuart Mill

Major works: *An Essay Concerning Human Understanding*, Locke, 1689; *A Treatise of Human Nature*, Hume, 1740

? Are we sure we can trust our senses?

'The rationalist imagines an imbecile-free society; the empiricist an imbecile-proof one, or even better, a rationalist-proof one.'

NASSIM NICHOLAS TALEB

Rationalism

The chief source of knowledge to a rationalist is reason. For this to work, reality has to have a logical structure, which can be revealed through reason alone. Mathematics is true, not because we see evidence of it but because it obeys the rules of logic, and rationalist philosophers attempt to extend that to the whole of reality. To do that they argue that some knowledge is *a priori*—in other words we are born knowing it—and our intuitions work as well as empirical evidence in showing the way to knowledge.

Leading figures: René Descartes, Baruch Spinoza, Gottfried Leibniz, Immanuel Kant

Major works: *Discourse on Method*, Descartes, 1637; *Monadology*, Leibniz, 1714; *Critique of Pure Reason*, Kant 1781

? Is thinking something true enough to make it true?

'When it is not in our power to determine what is true, we ought to follow what is most probable.'

RENÉ DESCARTES

THE SCHOOLS OF PHILOSOPHY ∗ 125

Platonism

Named for Plato and based on his theory of forms. The Greek term he used was *eidos* which is often translated as "idea" and informs branches such as idealism, which states that concepts exist only in the mind. However, Plato did not think his *eidos* are mind-dependent but are Forms that exist outside of time and space and are only accessible by reason. Reality is thus very different from what our senses tell us: Sensory beliefs are misleading, and tell us only about an unreal realm that is in constant flux. We must rely on our reason to know what is real and true. And those truths are unchanging and objective.

Leading figures: Plato

Major works: *The Republic*, Plato, c.380 BCE

? Is there a Form of Forms?

> '*In the world of knowledge, the essential Form of Good is the limit of our inquiries, and can barely be perceived.*'
>
> PLATO

Aristotelianism

Arguably the most influential philosophy through all of the Middle Ages, covering a range of topics from logic to biology and from physics to metaphysics. An Aristotelian believes that nature has a purpose, and is heading toward some end state. Human beings can come to know these truths about the world by sensory experience (combined with correct use of reason). In the modern era, these ideas are harnessed in the discussions of virtue ethics, where the good life is lived to maximize virtue, or good character, rather than to respond to duty, social rules, or contracts, as is the norm in other fields of ethics.

Leading figures: Aristotle, Avicenna, Averroes

Major works: *Organon*, Aristotle, c.50 BCE

? Does the Universe have a purpose?

> '*We are what we repeatedly do. Excellence, then, is not an act, but a habit.*'
>
> ARISTOTLE

Analytic philosophy

The dominant school in English-speaking countries in modern times, in contrast with the Continental philosophy that dominated the 20th century. The analytic school takes the analysis of language as key to unraveling philosophical mysteries, or at least to making progress on them. Practitioners focus on rigor, clarity of expression, and often a piecemeal approach to problems, as opposed to grand system-building that is often more characteristic of Continental approaches.

Leading figures: Bertrand Russell, Ludwig Wittgenstein

Major works: *Tractatus Logico-Philosophicus*, Wittgenstein, 1921

? Is there an answer to every question?

> '*The limits of my language means the limits of my world.*'
>
> LUDWIG WITTGENSTEIN

PHILOSOPHY CAN NEVER BE COMPLETE; HUMANITY WILL NEVER RUN OUT OF QUESTIONS—mainly because we can't agree on the answers! Here are a few open questions, some old and some new, that still require a thorough pondering.

Is the sky always blue?

Think back, what was the first thing you talked about with your parents? OK, you probably won't remember, and being fair it would have been a one-sided conversation, with your contribution being little more than a gurgle. After you got the hellos out of the way, Mom and Dad started to give you things to play with, saying their names and giving guidance on their proper use. Soon they would have added a bit of color, quite literally, by telling you the shades of the different objects that passed through your hands and before your eyes. This block is red, those leaves are green, that sky is blue, etc. As long as the weather holds out, the sky is always going to be that same color. We've agreed to call it blue. Other objects have the same color, roughly speaking. They are blue, too. Philosophers then ask if we are all seeing the same blue. We all use the same word, "blue" to refer to the sky's color. But the qualitative experience for each of us is private. I can't experience the world from the inside the way you do. Perhaps when you say "blue" you are having the experience of what I would call green, and vice versa. Could we ever find out for sure? All we have are our words to guide us, so if I try to check about our common uses of words, by asking you if the grass is green, you could agree with the word I use, but be experiencing a completely different set of qualities. Philosophers call this the "inverted spectrum problem." The *qualia*—the qualitative character of our experience—could be completely different for each of us and we'd never know! Or could we...?

We all see the same colors, but perhaps your colors are different to mine.

Should justice be based on luck?

A judge is preparing to sentence two people convicted of two identical although separate crimes. Let's say that they have stolen a loaf of bread out of another shopper's bag. Alfred was orphaned at birth and has had to look after himself for his whole life. He's down on his luck and has not eaten for days, hence the theft. In contrast, Bert has had a privileged upbringing, wanting for nothing. He stole the bread because he was late for an appointment and did not want to spare the time going to the store. The loss to both victims is equal, so is each crime morally equal too? Or does Alfred's bad luck at being orphaned mean his crime is not as bad as Bert's? Should the judge punish them equally or differently? Next the judge looks at the case of twins, Angie and Zöe. They were racing down an empty highway, breaking all the rules of the road. Being twins they are evenly matched, driving neck and neck in identical cars. Then a pedestrian crosses in front of the racing cars. Both twins brake at the same time. Angie hits a streetlight, knocking it over; Zöe kills the pedestrian. Should the judge punish the twins equally for their immoral actions? Or should she punish Zöe more than Angie because the consequence of her actions was worse?

Can you ever go bald?

A man is proud of his thick hair. But he soon finds that he sheds fibers occasionally—and they don't grow back! However, everyone agrees that he still has a full head of hair. Over the year more hairs fall out. At what point does he stop having a full head of hair? When does he become bald? Is there a point where the loss of one more hair will make the man bald? Surely 100,000 hairs makes a full head of hair, but removing one hair from the head would not disqualify it as a full head. Therefore, removing hairs one by one will always produce a full head of hair—how can one fewer hair make enough difference? That statement holds even when you get down to one hair left. And when you remove that one hair, you still have a full head of hair, by definition. Therefore, you can never go bald. This is nonsense, surely, but how do we relate quantitative concepts (the number of hairs) with qualitative ones (baldness).

What makes things funny?

A sense of humor is a universal human trait, but why do we sometimes laugh at things? And why do some people laugh at one thing when others are left stony-faced? The oldest theory is that we laugh to signal to ourselves that we feel superior to what (or whom) we are laughing at. This idea is as old as philosophy itself and is based on the fact that people don't like being laughed at—the act of laughter devalues the subject of the joke, and in this case it's you. However, surely the best jokes are more sophisticated than that? Perhaps laughter is an emotional safety valve. One theory suggests that emotions are our way of filling the gaps in reasoning and are put to use when we don't have the time or opportunity to think carefully about something. Our general emotional state—frightened … angry … lustful—ensures we muddle through a situation in the correct manner. Laughter, therefore, is a release of unneeded emotional energy, which dissipates as a physical energy. This is the relief theory: We laugh because we need to shed inappropriate emotions. The incongruity theory of humor is similar—just as other emotions are quick-start processes to deal with emergencies or difficult problems, happy laughter tackles our inability to understand incongruous situations—they're just a joke.

Is anything unexpected?

It's time for a surprise. Or is it? Let's say a wife forgets her husband's birthday—OK, that's too surprising. Let's say that a husband forgets his wife's birthday, and to make amends he says he will take her out to dinner in the next week (between Monday and Friday). He will make the arrangements and to add an element of surprise he will only tell her it's the big day at 7pm the night of the meal. The wife realizes that the meal won't be a surprise at all. She reasons that it can't take place on Friday night because after 7pm on Thursday she will not be surprised by a Friday night out. That means Thursday is out too, because Friday can never be a surprise, that makes Thursday the last possible day, and come 7pm Wednesday, there will be no surprise at all. The wife follows this reasoning to eliminate every day of the week. So much for her surprise! The wife concludes her husband will never take her out again—perhaps that is what he meant all along? She does not have time to brood for too long though. At 7pm on the Monday, he tells her tonight's the night. What a surprise!

Is time real?

What is the time? When you find out, please can you write it down because philosophers are having trouble figuring it out. Done that? What's your answer? Is it still correct? The truth is something as "simple" or ubiquitous as time is still a total mystery. Three possible natures of time have been proposed. Firstly, it is suggested that time is made up of future events, present events, and past events. Future events always become present events and then past events, and this explains why time travels in one direction and always will do. A second theory takes a slightly different view by simply ordering events according to whether they are earlier or later to each other. In both cases objects that existed a long time ago are just as real as the ones that exist right now. There is disagreement over whether future objects already exist. We'll have to wait and see. However, a third idea says that the only things that exist do so in the present. Every event destroys whatever caused it to happen and will be destroyed by any effect it results in. Turning the page means this page will cease to be part of reality—until you turn back to it again. This "presentist" theory is the best fit for our experience of time. After all, what else is reality other than what we perceive here and now? The past and the future only exist in our imaginations. However, the presentist concept does not tally with the time dilation effects of special relativity. This theory shows that events that appear to occur simultaneously to one observer happen at different times to another observer who is traveling at a much faster speed. So relativity breaks down the concept of the present. Does that make the presentist theory wrong? Or is special relativity wrong? Time might tell, or it might not.

Time always passes, but is it going past you, or are you going past it?

Does the mind's eye always match the real eye?

If a person who was blind from birth was able to differentiate a cube from a sphere by touch alone, would they be able to recognize the same objects by sight alone if they were made to see? This is the Molyneux problem, posed by William Molyneux to John Locke in the 17th century. Does the mind automatically translate understanding from touch into understanding from vision? In the 21st century, unlike the 17th, some people born blind can be made to see with the latest medical advances, so we may one day get an answer to this problem. The 17th-century hunch was that the answer is no, and modern results suggest that too: It takes a person several months to recognize shapes once their vision has been fixed.

These two shapes look very different but do they feel different in the same way?

The Great Philosophers

THE PEOPLE WHO ARE THE SUBJECT OF THIS BOOK are those who have thought the unthinkable—and in the process changed the way we can understand ourselves. Such people are very special. So, what makes a great philosopher? It is striking to note that philosophers come from all backgrounds— Ludwig Wittgenstein was the son of one the world's wealthiest men, while Jean-Jacques Rousseau was effectively fending for himself for most of his childhood. Let's take a look at some of the lives that shaped the history of philosophy.

Pythagoras

Born	c.570 BCE
Birthplace	Samos, Ionia, Greece
Died	c.500–490 BCE
Importance	Applied math to philosophy and science

Was Pythagoras real, a single person, or the personification of a school of thought? No one really knows. His life and works come to us from the accounts of others, in no small part from the writings of Plato. Tradition dictates that Pythagoras was born on the island of Samos. Having made an enemy of the tyrannical ruler of his home city, Pythagoras applied his legendary intelligence and got out of there. He traveled widely—perhaps as far as India—absorbing the math of Babylon, Egypt, and beyond, before settling in Croton in Italy, where he formed his Pythagorean community.

Thales of Miletus

Born	c.624 BCE
Birthplace	Miletus, western Turkey
Died	c.547–546 BCE
Importance	Father of Western philosophy

Ironically, for a figure who is credited as moving Western thought from the realm of myth to the rigor of empiricism, we have no direct evidence that Thales actually existed. It is thought he was taught by an Egyptian priest and spent time in Athens. The most concrete fact we have about him is that he is said to have been able to predict solar eclipses, and did so in a year that the Lydians and the Medes (both neighbors of Miletus) were at war with one another. A final battle between them was fought at Halys in 585 BCE and ended when "day was turned to night" by an eclipse. This is assumed to be the one predicted by Thales.

Siddhartha Gautama

Born	c.560 BCE
Birthplace	Lumbini, Nepal
Died	c.483 BCE
Importance	Founder of Buddhism

Compared to the biographies of the founders of other religions, the story of Gautama's life is a blur of contradictory accounts. Some style him as a prince but either way it is safe to say he enjoyed a privileged childhood. In taking his spiritual journey for which he is remembered, he abandoned his splendid lifestyle plus his wife and son—who no doubt remained in luxury. He is said to have reached enlightenment while meditating beneath a bodhi tree and spent the next 50 years or so touring India with a devoted entourage.

Confucius

Born	551 BCE
Birthplace	Qufu, China
Died	479 BCE
Importance	Underpinned Chinese morality and culture

This seminal Chinese thinker was born Kong Qiu. Only later was he elevated to Kongfuzi, meaning "Master Kong" in recognition of his works. It is this second name that has come down to us as the Latinized Confucius. Sent out to work at an early age to support his family after his father's death, Confucius rose to be a court administrator. Becoming disillusioned with the actions of the rulers he served, Confucius became an itinerant teacher. Much of his work survived through the Chinese oral tradition to be collated later by Confucian scholars.

Plato

Born	428/427 BCE
Birthplace	Athens, Greece
Died	348/347 BCE
Importance	Theory of "ideas" or "Forms"

Plato's place of birth is unknown, but he was certainly from an aristocratic family. As a young man he was taught by Socrates, and most of what we know of that great Athenian philosopher is from his pupil's accounts. After Socrates's execution, Plato founded a school called the Akademia, which has had a lasting impact on Western thought. The name, now so associated with schooling, probably derives from the previous owner of the land. One of its famous pupils was Aristotle. Plato's given name was Aristocles, but given his link to Aristotle, it is perhaps fortunate for history that he was nicknamed Plato, meaning "broad," by his wrestling teacher.

Socrates

Born	469 BCE
Birthplace	Athens, Greece
Died	399 BCE
Importance	The Socratic Method

Socrates is an enigma, even among philosophers. He did not found a school or leave any writings. We know he followed his father by training as a stonemason before fighting bravely in the Peloponnesian War. His father's bequest was enough for him to live modestly in Athens without working. However, his habit of humiliating powerful figures garnered him more enemies than followers. His reputation as one of history's greatest philosophers was created by his disciples, such as Plato, rather than through the efforts of Socrates himself.

Aristotle

Born	384 BCE
Birthplace	Stagira, northern Greece
Died	322 BCE
Importance	Key figure in early Western science

The son of the king's doctor, Aristotle was born into Macedonian aristocracy. As befitting his status, he finished his education in Athens, as a pupil of Plato. Aristotle's empirical approach gave him a broad legacy in the sciences and philosophy and superseded that of his master and of any other Greek philosopher. His science is often mentioned more for its errors than true discoveries, which were being corrected for many centuries after his death. Nevertheless, Aristotle left us works that gave intellectuals from as far afield as Turkmenistan and Ireland pause for thought for two millennia.

Hypatia of Alexandria

Born	c.355 CE
Birthplace	Alexandria, Egypt
Died	March 415 CE
Importance	Last philosopher of Classical era

Hypatia was a woman who made her mark at a time when women seldom made it into a classroom, let alone into history books. Hypatia's father was the last head of the great Library of Alexandria, and so she had the best education from the start. She is credited with the invention of the hydrometer, a glass and mercury weight that floated in liquids, but in more general terms she was the last in the long line of scholars in the Classical Hellenic tradition. She was murdered and her body butchered by a crowd of Christians who objected to her teaching Plato's philosophy, which was seen as heretical.

Boëthius

Born	c.470
Birthplace	Rome, Italy
Died	525
Importance	Omniscience and free will

Anicius Boëthius was born into a noble Roman family, but orphaned at an early age. This proved no particular hindrance, since he was taken in by friends, and the boy was afforded the best education. He went on to a life of scholarship, translating and critiquing the works of Aristotle. By adulthood, the Ostrogoths had toppled the Romans and taken power in his native Italy. He then became an advisor to the Goth king Theodoric, and proved to be less good at politics: He was falsely accused of treason and sentenced to death. He wrote his greatest work, *The Consolation of Philosophy*, while awaiting execution.

Augustine of Hippo

Born	November 13, 345
Birthplace	Thagaste (now in Algeria)
Died	August 28, 430
Importance	Christian Platonist

Augustine was North African by birth but was a Roman citizen. His mother was a Christian but his father was a pagan, following the old Greco-Roman gods. Augustine converted to Christianity in his midthirties and spent the last third of his life as the Bishop of Hippo in Roman North Africa. In his final days, the city was besieged by the Vandals in their conquest of the Roman Empire. Augustine is said to have miraculously healed the sick during the siege—for which he was made a saint—before dying himself days before the city fell.

Avicenna

Born	980
Birthplace	Bukhara, Uzbekhistan
Died	1037
Importance	Islamic scholar

Known as Ibn Sina in Arabic, Avicenna proved to be a bright spark from an early age, outwitting his teachers in science and philosophy. The story goes that he administered to the health needs of the local emir while still in his teens. One benefit of this position was that Avicenna was given access to the royal library, allowing him to spread his sphere of interest to encompass physics and politics,

accruing considerable wealth in the process. In the end he wrote 200 books himself, and would have produced more if he had not been poisoned by one of his servants.

Rumi

Born	September 30, 1207
Birthplace	Balkh, Persia
Died	December 17, 1273
Importance	Leading Sufi

With the full name Jalal ad-Din Muhammad Rumi, this Islamic scholar is also referred to as Mawlana, meaning "Our Guide." Tradition suggested that his family was descended from Abu Bakr, the first Caliph, although that assertion is now largely discredited. Rumi grew up on the northeastern edge of the Islamic world, and an invading Mongol horde forced his family to move to the security of what is now Turkey. It was here that the young Rumi was exposed to the mysticism of Sufism. He remained there for the rest of his life, rising to become a leader of a Sufi order, the Mawlawi, which survives to this day.

Thomas Aquinas

Born	January 28, 1225
Birthplace	Roccasecca, Italy
Died	March 7, 1274
Importance	Christian Aristotelian

Thomas Aquinas belonged to a minor lineage of a noble family. While his brothers looked for advancement in the military, Thomas opted to join the Dominicans, at the time a newly formed Christian order with a reputation for intellect. Aquinas studied in Cologne, Germany, under Albertus Magnus, who proved to be a lasting influence, and then went on to have two stints as master of theology at the Paris university (one of the first in Europe). In 1273, he suffered a seizure, which was interpreted as a vision, which made him renounce his life's works as "mere straw." He died the year after.

Niccolò Machiavelli

Born	May 3, 1469
Birthplace	Florence, Italy
Died	June 21, 1527
Importance	Political philosopher

Few men achieve the enormous honor of having their names transformed into adjectives. Machiavelli is one of those few, although many will be forgiven for not having made the connection between him and the term Machiavellian. This word first appeared about a century after his death—it means the "employment of cunning and duplicity." By accident or cunning design, we know nothing of Machiavelli's early life. Almost the first we hear of him is from 1498, when he was a Florentine diplomat, who crisscrossed Italy as a go-between for rival powers. However, his political career was stymied by the rise of the Medicis in Florence and he spent the remaining 15 years of his life writing about securing political power—despite failing to do so himself.

Francis Bacon

Born	January 22, 1561
Birthplace	London, England
Died	April 9, 1626
Importance	Scientific method

Francis Bacon is remembered for formulating the scientific method. He was not a scientist but a lawyer, politician, and courtier to Queen Elizabeth I and King James I, her successor in 1603. (The highest rank of British lawyers is QC, or Queen's Counsel. This honor was created specifically for Bacon to salve his ire at missing out on better promotions.) At the end of his life, Bacon suffered a spectacular fall from grace, accused of corruption, which saw him spend time in the Tower of London. He spent his last few years out of the public gaze, and after his death gossip spread that he had been the king's lover.

Thomas Hobbes

Born	April 5, 1588
Birthplace	Westport, England
Died	December 4, 1679
Importance	Physicalism

Thomas Hobbes was affected by world events even before he was born. When his mother heard that a Spanish fleet was approaching the English coast, she gave birth—in the later words of Hobbes—to "twins; myself and fear." Hobbes's father was an irascible vicar, who lost his job and promptly abandoned his family. Luckily, Hobbes was supported by his wealthy uncle. Hobbes became the tutor of the Earl of Devonshire, and traveled with him to meet the greatest minds of his generation, including Kepler and Galileo. Hobbes inherited his father's ability to offend, and in later life he was sometimes forced to flee from powerful figures.

John Locke

Born	August 29, 1632
Birthplace	Wrington, England
Died	October 28, 1704
Importance	Theory of knowledge

John Locke was the son of a lawyer, and made the most of his middle-class upbringing, excelling at Westminster School in London and Oxford University. His early career was in the new field of science, where he assisted Robert Boyle, said to be the founding father of chemistry. Later Locke turned to political discourse, writing about human rights and society. As a result, he had to flee England twice, finally returning for good after the Glorious Revolution of 1688. It was in this later stage of his life that Locke worked for the government and wrote his most famous work on human understanding.

René Descartes

Born	March 31, 1596
Birthplace	La Haye, Touraine, France
Died	February 11, 1650
Importance	Rationalist

Descartes made contributions to physics and math as well as philosophy. His laws of motion were amended by Isaac Newton while he is responsible for the graphs that students plot in math classes to this day. Descartes was a Roman Catholic but as an adult he chose to live in Dutch territories, even serving in the army. In the Netherlands, Protestantism was to the fore but so too was religious tolerance. Descartes shelved his first major work, *Treatise on the World*, after his contemporary Galileo was put on trial for heresy. However, much of this work later found its way into his masterwork, *Discours de la Méthode*.

David Hume

Born	April 26, 1711
Birthplace	Edinburgh, Scotland
Died	August 25, 1776
Importance	Leading figure of Scottish Enlightenment

David Hume showed his intelligence earlier than most. He began his university career in Edinburgh at the tender age of 12. By his midtwenties he had worked himself into a nervous breakdown and made a fresh start in France. The change did him good, and it was here that he wrote his *Treatise of Human Nature*, for which he is most remembered today. After many happier years back in Edinburgh, he was eventually appointed as an ambassador in Paris where his reputation as a philosopher flowered. Hume's final work on religion was so controversial its publication was delayed until after his death.

Jean-Jacques Rousseau

Born	June 28, 1712
Birthplace	Geneva, Switzerland
Died	July 2, 1778
Importance	Social contract theory

Things did not start well for Jean-Jacques Rousseau. His mother died a few days after his birth. By the time the boy was ten, his father had effectively abandoned him, fleeing Geneva with his sister-in-law, leaving his son in the care of an uncle. Rousseau ran away from school at the age of 15 and learned to support himself. He lived in Italy and France but when his controversial philosophy led to arrest warrants, he fled to England. However, Rousseau preferred to risk imprisonment and returned to France under a false name shortly after. He became something of a celebrity in his final decade but lived as a recluse due to depression.

Immanuel Kant

Born	April 22, 1724
Birthplace	Königsberg, Prussia (now Kaliningrad, Russia)
Died	February 12, 1804
Importance	Author of *Critique of Pure Reason*

For a man who had such far-reaching effects on how humans reason, it is ironic that Immanuel Kant never traveled more than a few miles from his home city of Königsberg. He was a man of habits: It was said that his neighbors set their clocks by the time he took his daily walks. His childhood was  humble and pious, although this did not stop Kant from questioning religion from an early age. He entered the local university at the age of 16, and he stayed there for the rest of his career. His middle years were outwardly inactive, but belied a vigorous inner life that resulted in the theory of transcendental idealism in the 1780s.

Adam Smith

Born	June 5, 1723
Birthplace	Kirkcaldy, Scotland
Died	July 17, 1790
Importance	Founder of modern economics

There is a story that Adam Smith was kidnapped by a gypsy woman at the age of four. Fortunately, he was returned to his mother, as one commentator said, "he would have made a poor gypsy." History shows that he made a good philosopher, with the capitalist engine that powers the global economy, such as it is, being built on his ideas. Smith showed his acumen early, becoming a full professor by the age of 27. He then became the private tutor of a Scottish aristocrat, affording him the luxury of touring Europe. On his return to Scotland he spent ten years writing the *Wealth of Nations*.

Edmund Burke

Born	January 12, 1729
Birthplace	Dublin, Ireland
Died	July 9, 1797
Importance	Political philosopher

Edmund Burke's philosophy went hand in hand with his political career. He formed a debating society at Dublin's Trinity College, which is now the College Historical Society, the oldest undergraduate group in the world. His debating skills were meant to serve a law career in London, but he soon dropped out to become a man of letters, before entering the British Parliament at the age of 36. He was quickly recognized as a formidable orator. However, his most famous saying, "The only thing necessary for evil to triumph is for good men to do nothing," is not found anywhere in his writings.

Mary Wollstonecraft

Born	April 27, 1759
Birthplace	London, England
Died	September 10, 1797
Importance	Founding figure in feminism

Mary Wollstonecraft was one of seven children in an unhappy family. Her father squandered his fortune and was violent. Mary became her mother's protector, sleeping across her bedroom door to block his way. In adult life she continued to break social norms, moving to France weeks before it was thrown into revolution. She had a child with an American adventurer, and attempted suicide twice after he left her, despite finding fame through her writing at this point. She found love again back in London but died giving birth to her second child (Mary Shelley, author of *Frankenstein*).

John Stuart Mill

Born	May 20, 1806
Birthplace	London, England
Died	May 8, 1873
Importance	Utilitarianism

John Stuart Mill was educated by his father, who was James Mill, a Scottish philosopher. So it is little wonder that the son ended up in the pantheon of English philosophers. His education was intense—he was learning ancient Greek at  the age of three, and by the age of 20 he suffered a nervous collapse. Mill dropped out of college and went to work in India, not returning to England for 30 years. His writing career began in the east but his philosophical masterworks were penned in later life, when Mill also served as a member of parliament.

Georg Hegel

Born	August 27, 1770
Birthplace	Stuttgart, Germany
Died	November 14, 1831
Importance	Leading figure in idealism

Despite being a bright student—he had mastered the rudiments of Latin by the age of five—Hegel could not afford to pursue an academic career. After his first degree (in theology), he worked as a tutor for almost a decade before an inheritance allowed him to rejoin his university friend (and now philosopher) Friedrich Schelling at the University of Jena. Napolean's eastward conquests forced Hegel to flee, taking with him the draft of his masterwork, *Phenomenology of Spirit*.  He then made ends meet working as a teacher and journalist before becoming a professor of philosophy.

Søren Kierkegaard

Born	May 5, 1813
Birthplace	Copenhagen, Denmark
Died	November 11, 1855
Importance	Existentialism

Kierkegaard was a leading figure in the Danish Golden Age, but personally he was said to have a less than sparkling outlook on life, prone to bouts of depression. This is evident in his work, which is nothing if not bleak. At Copenhagen's university, he skipped his theology lectures to take philosophy classes, and upon inheriting a small fortune, he became a professional  philosopher. He famously fell in love with an aristocratic Danish girl, but backed out of the engagement, saying he was too miserable to be a good husband. A little more than a decade later, Kierkegaard collapsed into a coma in the street, perhaps due to a childhood head injury, and never woke up.

Karl Marx

Born	May 5, 1818
Birthplace	Trier, Germany
Died	March 14, 1883
Importance	Communism

If success is counted in statues, then Karl Marx is by far the most successful philosopher in history. In the 1980s two dozen countries followed his manifesto (but barely five do so now). Marx's ideology came from experience. He was exiled from Germany for promoting democratic government, he witnessed a revolution at first hand (it failed), and he lived out the rest of his life in poverty in  London. He is buried in Highgate Cemetery. Only 11 people came to the funeral although his monument now gets daily visits. (Be warned, he is actually buried around the corner.)

Friedrich Nietzsche

Born	October 15, 1844
Birthplace	Röcken, Germany
Died	August 25, 1900
Importance	Challenged traditional morality

Nietzsche came from a staunchly Lutheran family and was brought up in a household of women—his father and brother died when he was young. His abiding attitude was that although faith led to peace, inquiry led to truth, and he chose the latter. When a promising career in the Prussian military was cut short by an injury, the young Nietzsche settled on intellectual pursuits. However, illness continued to plague  him. In 1889 he suffered a mental collapse in Turin—it is often stated that it was precipitated by witnessing a horse being flogged in the street—and never worked again.

William James

Born	January 11, 1842
Birthplace	New York City, USA
Died	August 26, 1910
Importance	Pragmatism and psychology

William is not the most famous member of the James family. His brother Henry James was the author of *The Portrait of a Lady*, *The Turn of the Screw*, and other famous American novels. His father was a notable theologian while his sister is also remembered for her diary. (This relates her battle with illness and hints at an incestuous attraction  to William.) The young William began with ambitions to be a painter but opted for medicine instead. After graduating he became interested in psychology (he suffered mental illness himself). Philosophy, which he taught at Harvard until 1907, was his third career.

John Dewey

Born	October 20, 1859
Birthplace	Burlington, Vermont, USA
Died	June 1, 1952
Importance	Pragmatist and educationalist

After a short career as a teacher, Dewey took further degrees in psychology and philosophy and became a academic, initially at the newly formed University of Chicago. After a distinguished career, he took a sabbatical in Japan and China, just as the colonial powers were ceding  territory on mainland China to the Japanese as a part of the World War I settlement. That inspired Dewey to become an advocate for democratic interventions in China to counter the lure of communism from the newly formed USSR. History reflects his warnings went unheeded.

Bertrand Russell

Born	May 18, 1872
Birthplace	Trelleck, Wales
Died	February 2, 1970
Importance	Leading philosopher of mathematics

Born into a wealthy and influential British family that was active in the political elite from before the days of Henry VIII, Russell inherited an earldom. Despite his privileged upbringing, the young Bertrand was a lonely youth and  considered suicide. However, he found his calling in math and philosophy, and had become a figure of world stature by his thirties. But this was not the end of his career. Russell was a staunch pacifist and was a leading antinuclear campaigner in the 1950s, frequently being arrested during demonstrations and was even imprisoned.

Martin Heidegger

Born	September 26, 1889
Birthplace	Messkirch, Germany
Died	May 26, 1976
Importance	Phenomenology

 Martin Heidegger's childhood was spent in rural Germany, where his parents were church officials. They could not afford to send him to university, so the young Martin was enrolled in a Jesuit seminary. However, he was thrown out for having a heart condition (deemed to be psychosomatic). After reading the work of Edmund Husserl, Martin chose another path and began a meteoric rise as a philosophy lecturer, becoming a professor at Marburg and then taking the chair of his mentor Husserl at Freiberg. In 1933, he joined the Nazi Party. After the war, he was barred from teaching until the early 1950s.

Ludwig Wittgenstein

Born	April 26, 1889
Birthplace	Vienna, Austria
Died	April 29, 1951
Importance	Logic and language

Ludwig came from a family of high achievers: His father Karl was a superrich tycoon; the Wittgensteins were the second wealthiest family in the Austro-Hungarian Empire. Brother Paul was the world's best one-handed piano player (he'd lost the other in World War I). Ludwig wanted to be an engineer and moved to England to study. It was there that he became interested in philosophy, under the auspices of Bertrand Russell. In World War I, Ludwig was taken prisoner by the Italians and wrote the early drafts of his eclectic *Tractus Logico-Philosophicus* in captivity.

Karl Popper

Born	July 28, 1902
Birthplace	Vienna, Austria
Died	September 17, 1994
Importance	Philosophy of science

Karl Popper was a late bloomer. As a young man he dabbled with psychology, obtaining a PhD; was apprenticed as a cabinetmaker; and was a Marxist activist. By 1929, he had qualified as a math teacher, but soon recognized that his Jewish roots could prove to be a major problem as the Nazis began to rise in popularity. He  spent his spare time writing his first book, which would be his ticket out of Austria. In 1937, he won a place at Canterbury University in New Zealand before moving to the London School of Economics where he spent the rest of his life.

Jean-Paul Sartre

Born	June 21, 1905
Birthplace	Paris, France
Died	April 15, 1980
Importance	Existentialist

This archetypal French philosopher rivals Sherlock Holmes as the most famous pipesmoker in the world. Brought up by his mother and grandmother, Jean-Paul Sartre was bullied at school but proved to be a gifted student. He won a place at Paris's École Normale Supérieure, an elite college that dates back to the  French Revolution. There he met his lifelong companion, Simone de Beauvoir. He was a professor in Le Havre for most of the 1930s. After the surrender to Germany in 1940, Sartre joined the Resistance, and after the war he became a leading political radical, with a large popular following.

Jacques Derrida

Born	July 15, 1930
Birthplace	El Biar, Algeria
Died	October 9, 2004
Importance	Deconstructionism

Born in the then-French colony of Algeria, Derrida was an ethnic North African Jew. His education was disrupted by the anti-Semitic laws of France's Nazi-controlled Vichy government. He was expelled from high school, and instead of going to the Jewish school, Derrida skipped lessons to concentrate  on soccer. In his late teens he was inspired to leave sports behind and concentrate on philosophy. After studying in the USA he began a teaching career in Paris in 1960. It was in this decade that his major works were written. The last 20 years or so of his life were spent teaching in California.

Simone de Beauvoir

Born	January 9, 1908
Birthplace	Paris, France
Died	April 14, 1986
Importance	Feminist

Known for her fiction as much as her philosophy, Simone de Beauvoir was a religious child. However, she lost her faith at the age of 14. She took math and philosophy at the Sorbonne, meeting her life partner Jean-Paul Sartre while taking courses at the nearby École Normale Supérieure. He offered a "two-year lease" instead of marriage, but they  stayed together for a lot longer even if they never married. In the 1930s and 40s, she was an academic, where she is said to have frequently seduced her female students. Later, writing became her main occupation.

Richard Rorty

Born	October 4, 1931
Birthplace	New York City, USA
Died	June 8, 2007
Importance	Metaphilosophy

 Richard Rorty learned to say what he thought at an early age. His parents were radical political activists, who supported Leon Trotsky, a Russian socialist on the run from Stalin's assassins at the time. (They finally got him in 1940.) Rorty whizzed through his education, gaining a PhD by the age of 25, and, after two years in the army, became a philosophy lecturer. He struggled with mental-health issues in the 1960s while working at Princeton. His most famous work was completed while working at the University of Virginia.

BIBLIOGRAPHY AND OTHER RESOURCES

Books

Baggini, Julian and Jeremy Stangroom (eds.). *Great Thinkers A–Z*. London and New York: Continuum, 2004.

Blackburn, Simon. *The Oxford Dictionary of Philosophy*. Oxford: Oxford University Press, 1996.

—*Think: A Compelling Introduction to Philosophy*. Oxford: Oxford University Press, 1999.

Borchert, Donald M. (ed. in chief). *Encyclopedia of Philosophy*. Farmington Hills: Macmillan, 2006.

Burnyeat, Myles and Ted Honderich. *Philosophy as it is*. London: Penguin, 1993.

Chalton, Nicola (ed.). *Philosophers: Extraordinary People who Altered the Course of History*. London: Basement Press, 2008.

Collinson, Diane. *Fifty Major Philosophers*. London: Routledge, 1987.

Craig, E. (ed.). The *Routledge Encyclopedia of Philosophy*. London: Routledge, 1998.

Grayling, A. (ed.). *Philosophy Vol. 1: A Guide Through the Subject*. Oxford: Oxford University Press, 1998.

—*Philosophy Vol 2: Further Through the Subject*. Oxford: Oxford University Press, 1998.

Hollis, Martin. *An Invitation to Philosophy*. Oxford and New York: Blackwell, 1985.

Honderich, Ted (ed.). *The Oxford Companion to Philosophy*. Oxford: Oxford University Press, 1995.

Irwin, William, Mark T. Conard and Aeon J. Skoble (eds.). *The Simpsons and Philosophy: The D'oh! of Homer*. Chicago: Open Court, 2001.

Murdoch, Iris. *Metaphysics as a Guide to Morals*. London: Chatto, 1992.

Nagel, Thomas. *What Does It All Mean?* New York: Oxford University Press, 1987.

Rohmann, Chris. *The Dictionary of Important Ideas and Thinkers*. London: Hutchinson, 2001.

Russell, Bertrand. *A History of Western Philosophy*. London: George Allen & Unwin, 1946.

Smart, Ninian. *World Philosophies*. London: Routledge, 1999.

Stokes, Philip. *Philosophy: The Great Thinkers*. London: Arcturus, 2007.

Warburton, Nigel. *Philosophy: The Basics*. London: Routledge, 2012.

Warburton, Nigel. *A Little History of Philosophy*. London: Yale, 2012.

Various authors. "Arguments of the Philosophers." Routledge.

—"Blackwell Philosopher Dictionaries." Blackwell.

—"Cambridge Companions." Cambridge University Press.

—"The Philosophy Book." Dorling Kindersley.

—"Oxford Readings in Philosophy." Oxford University Press.

—"Routledge Philosophy GuideBooks." Routledge.

Websites

Ask Philosophers www.AskPhilosophers.org

In Our Time Philosophy Archive, BBC Radio 4 podcasts www.bbc.co.uk

Internet Encyclopedia of Philosophy www.iep.utm.edu

Routledge Encyclopedia of Philosophy Online www.rep.routledge.com

Stanford Encyclopedia of Philosophy www.plato.stanford.edu

The Wittgenstein Archives at the University of Bergen www.wab.uib.no

Apps

AskPhil for iPad/iPhone and Android

Introducing Philosophy for Android

Philosophy Bites for iPad/iPhone

Radical Philosophy for iPad/iPhone

Archives

Francis Bacon correspondence and papers, Lambeth Palace Library, London, UK, www.lambethpalacelibrary.org

Edmund Burke manuscripts, Sheffield Archives, Sheffield, South Yorkshire, UK, www.sheffield.gov.uk/archives

Jacques Derrida Papers, Critical Theory Archive, University of California Irvine, USA, www.ucispace.lib.uci.edu

René Descartes Papers, Institut de France, Paris, France, www.institut-de-france.fr

John Dewey Papers, Southern Illinois University, Carbondale, Illinois, USA, www.archives.lib.siu.edu

Hegel's House Museum, Stuttgart, Germany, www.stuttgart-tourist.de/en/a-hegel-house

Martin Heidegger Archives, German Literature Archive, Marbach, Germany, www.dla-marbach.de

David Hume Manuscripts, Royal Society of Edinburgh, Edinburgh, Scotland, UK, www.royalsoced.org.uk

William James Papers, Houghton Library, Harvard University, Cambridge, Massachusetts, USA, www.hcl.harvard.edu/libraries/houghton

Søren Kierkegaard Archive, Royal Library, Copenhagen, Denmark, www.kb.dk/en

John Locke papers, Lovelace Collection, Bodleian Library, University of Oxford, Oxford, UK, www.bodleian.ox.ac.uk

Karl Marx/Friedrich Engels Papers, International Institute of Social History, Amsterdam, The Netherlands, www.socialhistory.org/en

John Stuart Mill papers, Mill-Taylor Papers, London School of Economics, London, UK, www.lse.ac.uk

Friedrich Nietzsche Archive, Weimar Classics Foundation, Weimar, Germany, www.klassik-stiftung.de/en

Karl Popper Archive, University of Klagenfurt Library, Austria, www.uni-klu.ac.at

Karl Popper Papers, Hoover Institution Archives, Stanford University, California, USA, www.hoover.org

Richard Rorty Papers, Critical Theory Archive, University of California Irvine, USA, www.ucispace.lib.uci.edu

Jean-Jacques Rousseau Collections, Bibliothèque de Genève, Geneva, Switzerland, www.ville-ge.ch/bge; Jean-Jacques Rousseau Society of Geneva, Switzerland, www.sjjr.ch; Jean-Jacques Rousseau Association, Neuchâtel, Switzerland, www.bpun.unine.ch; Neuchâtel Public and University Library, Neuchâtel, Switzerland, www.bpun.unine.ch

Museum of Jean-Jacques Rousseau, Montmorency, France, museejjrousseau.montmorency.fr

Bertrand Russell Papers, McMaster University Library, Hamilton, Canada, www.library.mcmaster.ca

Ludwig Wittgenstein Papers, Wren Library, Trinity College, University of Cambridge, UK, www.trin.cam.ac.uk

Mary Wollstonecraft correspondence and papers Bodleian Library, University of Oxford, Oxford, UK, www.bodleian.ox.ac.uk

INDEX

Cataloging-in-Publication Data has been applied for and may be obtained from the Library of Congress.

ISBN 978-0-9853230-7-3

Series Concept and Direction: Jeanette Limondjian
Design: Bradbury and Williams
Editor: Meredith MacArdle
Proofreader: Marion Dent
Picture Research: Louise Thomas, www.cashou.com
Consultant: Dr. Eric M. Rubinstein
Jacket Design: Invisible design

Publisher's Note: While every effort has been made to ensure that the information herein is complete and accurate, the publishers and authors make no representations or warranties either expressed or implied of any kind with respect to this book to the reader. Neither the authors nor the publisher shall be liable or responsible for any damage, loss, or expense of any kind arising out of information contained in this book. The thoughts or opinions expressed in this book represent the personal views of the authors and not necessarily those of the publisher. Further, the publisher takes no responsibility for third party websites or their content.

SHELTER HARBOR PRESS
603 West 115th Street Suite 163
New York, New York 10025

For sales in the U.S. and Canada, please contact info@shelterharborpress.com

For sales in the UK and Europe, please contact info@worthpress.co.uk

Printed and bound in China by Imago.

10 9 8 7 6 5 4 3

PICTURE CREDITS
BOOK

Alamy/19th era 57 centre right; AF Archive 117 top right; Ancient Art & Architecture Collection Ltd. 132 top left; The Art Archive 31 below left, 39 centre left, 40 below centre, 52 below, 82; The Art Gallery Collection 29; Bildagentur-online Historical Collection 122 centre right; Design Pics Inc. 100 centre right; DPA Picture Alliance Archive/Stephanie Pilick 117 below left; GL Archive 2 below, 22; Peter Horree 133 top left; Geoff A. Howard 81 below right; Image Asset Management Ltd. 6 below left, 25 below left, 40 top right; INTERFOTO 77 centre left; Geraint Lewis 74; North Winds Picture Archives 21 below right; Painting 48 top right; Pictorial Press Ltd. 77 below right, 138 below left; Damiano Poli 95 centre right; Prisma Archivo 3 below, 17 centre right, 30 below left, 120 top right; ZUMA Press, Inc. 107 below left. **Archives Gallimard**/85. **Jaime Ardiles-Arce**/26 below left. **from Francis Bacon, _The Advancement of Learning_, 1640**/41 below right. **Public Domain Bible Development Project, Images of Saints Collection**/32 centre right. **from Richard Chiswell, _Baconiana_, 1679**/133 below right. **from H. Colburn, _The Narrative of the Surveying Voyages of HMS Adventure and Beagles_, 1838**/64 below. **from Nicolaus Copernicus, _De revolutionibus orbium coelestium_, 1543**/88. **Corbis**/137 below right; adoc-photos 124, 136 centre; Bettmann 19 below right, 79 below right, 87 top left, 109 below right, 120 below centre, 130 below left, 137 centre right, 137 below left, 138 top left; Stefano Bianchetti 31 centre right, 51 below right; Christie's Images 134 below right; Design Pics/Ken Welsh 27 centre left; DPA/Fred Stein 138 top right; EPA/Susanne Lindholm 109 centre left; Christopher Felver 121; Hulton-Deutsch Collection 139 below left; JAI/Nigel Pavitt 113 below; Mimmo Jodice 18; Lebrecht Music & Arts 58 top right; James Leynse 139 top right; Colin McPherson 123; Reuters/Henry Romero 105; Reuters/Benoit Tessier 115 below right; Sunset Boulevard 71 top left; Sygma/Apis/James Andanson 139 top left; Sygma/Apis/Michel Ginfray 5 top right, 83 below; Sygma/Patrick Chauvel 83 top right; Sygma/Julio Donoso 100 below left; Sygma/J.P. Laffont 103 centre left; George W. Wright 111 cr. **Jacques-Louis David, _The Death of Socrates_. 1787**/21 top left. **from René Descartes, _Médiations Métaphysiques_, 1647**/43 top left. **Dreamstime.com**/Georgios Kollidas 62 top right, 119; Stefanos Kyriazis 23 top right. **Mary Evans Picture Library**/11 below right, 16 centre right, 47 below right, 66 below right, 128, 130 centre, 136 below right; AISA Media 13 below left, 53 below left; Everett Collection 71 below, 103 top right; Grenville Collins 34 centre left; Grosvenor Prints 53 top right; Iberfoto 33 centre right, 52 top left; INTERFOTO 12, 72, 79 top right; Interfoto Agentur 38 below left; Douglas McCarthy 37 below right; National Magazine Company 84 top right; Photo Researchers 122 top left; Rue des Archives 69 top left, 84 below left, 89 centre left, 90 top right; SZ Photo 125; Roger Viollet 135 top left. **Getty**/AFP/Yoshikazu Tsuno 107 centre right; David Levenson 138 below right; Time Life Pictures/Marty Katz 139 below right. **from Thomas Hobbes, _Leviathan_, 1651**/6 top right, 42 top right. **from Robert Hooke, _Micrographia_, 1665**/45 top right. **from James Hutton, _Theory of the Earth_, 1795**/49. **iStockphoto.com**/131 centre left. **Library of Congress, Washington, D.C.**/23 below, 50, 54, 59, 75 top left, 77 top right, 97, 132 below right, 134 top left, 134 centre right, 134 below left, 135 below left, 136 top left, 136 below centre, 137 top left; Dorothea Lange/U.S. Farm Security Administration/Office of War Information 87 below. **from Gottfried Leibniz, _Essais de Théodicée sur la bonté de Dieu_, 1734**/47 top left. **NASA**/ESA, and the Hubble SM4 ERO Team 9 top left; Johnson Space Center 110 top right. **National Undersea Research Program (NURP) Collection/NOAA**/24. **PHGCOM**/licensed under the Creative Commons Attribution-Share Alike 3.0 Unported License (http://commons.wikimedia.org/wiki/File:TheBuddhaAndVajrapaniGandhara2ndCentury.jpg) 15 top right. **Private Collection**/37 top left, 38 top right, 41 top left, 43 below, 51 top left, 60, 75 centre right, 98. **REX**/Peter Brooker

114. **Science Photo Library**/Royal Astronomical Society 2 background, 13 centre right. **Shutterstock.com**/92; Antonio Abrigani 58 below; Zvonimir Atletic 132 below centre; Ziga Camernik 101 below (droplet); Hung Chung Chih 130 below right; Sharon Day 80 centre right; Zhu Difeng 106 top left (3); Claudio Divizia 79 centre left; Everett Collection 67 top centre; Angelo Gilardelli 9 centre left below; Jorg Hackemann 81 top right; LeshaBu 93; Mostovyi Sergii Igorevich 63; Kamira 26 top right, 131 below left; Zoran Karapancev 102; Malgorzata Kistryn 62 below left; Krafete 46; J-R Lelde 27 below; mg1408 73; Motordigitaal 20; Nicku 55 top centre, Nic Neufeld 106 top left (1); Pocky Gallery 106 top left (4); Reed 99 top right; 70; Tamas Schrek 113 top right; Scorpp 110 below right; Renata Sedmakova 35; SeDmi 45 below left; Fedor Selivanov 90 below centre; Somchaij top left (2); Andrey Tiyk 101 below (shower); D. Topal 99 below centre; Ungor 9 centre left; Rob Wilson 9 centre left above; Yadom 15 below left; Ko Yo 34 below right. **Thinkstock.com**/Aomnet7 9 below left; Hemera 11 top right, 11 centre left; iStockphoto 4 below left, 10, 14, 16 left, 27 top right, 33 below right, 39 below, 44 below left, 48 below left, 48 below centre (left), 48 below centre (right), 48 below right, 56 below left, 75 below left, 76, 80 below left, 94 below, 95 below centre, 96 centre right, 104, 108, 127 top left, 127 below right, 131 below right, 135 centre; Jakub Krechowicz 4-5 background; Vladislav Ociacia 7 background, 116; Photos.com 36, 44 top right, 56 top right, 57 below left, 64 centre right, 65, 66 centre left, 67 below right, 68 top left, 68 below right, 69 below right, 131 centre right, 132 top centre, 133 below left, 135 below right. **from Didacus Valdes, _Retorica Christiana_, 1579**/25 top right. **Roy Williams**/61, 78, 94 top right, 101 below, 112, 115 top right, 126, 129 top left. **The Yorck Project/Zenodot Verlagsgellschaft mbH**/licensed under the GNU Free Documentation License 28, 30 centre right.

TIMELINES

Alamy/Bible Land Pictures; Image Asset Management Ltd.; Lebrecht Music & Arts; Pictorial Press Ltd. **Corbis**/adoc-photos; Bettmann; BPI; Dan Joyce; Reuters/Kyodo; Sygma/Julio Donoso. **Mary Evans Picture Library**/Everett Collection; Robert Hunt Collection; London Fire Brigade; Iberfoto; INTERFOTO; Photo Researchers; Rue des Archives. **Library of Congress, Washington, D.C.**/George Grantham Bain Collection; Brady-Handy Collection; Carol M. Highsmith Archive; U.S. Navy. **NASA**/Hubble Space Telescope. **Private Collection**. Shutterstock.**com**/Kamira; KUCO; Radoslaw Lecyk. **from André Thevet, _Les Vrais Portraits et Vies des Hommes Illustres_, 1584**. **Thinkstock.com**/Digital Vision; Hemera; istockphoto; Photos.com.

Publisher's note: Every effort has been made to trace copyright holders and seek permission to use illustrative material. The publishers wish to apologize for any inadvertent errors or omissions and would be glad to rectify these in future editions.